Walking in God's Will i
or check-all-the-boxes m........ .... word
and embrace his grace so you can live out his will both for his glory
and your good. I wouldn't trust any book on this subject that doesn't
address humility and suffering. Costi covers both, with remarkable
insight.

—Randy Alcorn, *New York Times* bestselling author;
founder and director, Eternal Perspective Ministries

Doing the will of God is the foundational and essential pursuit of
Christian living. Yet to fulfill it, one must first discern His will (Rom.
12:2). Costi Hinn helps us do just that in this clear and compelling book.

—John MacArthur, pastor, Grace Community Church, Sun Valley,
California; chancellor, The Master's University and Seminary

There are few issues Christians wrestle with more frequently and more
earnestly than the matter of God's will for their lives. And there are
few issues for which there is so much teaching that is unhelpful or even
unbiblical. That's where this book is so important. It goes straight to
the Bible to teach how Christians can confidently know and do God's
will for their lives. I am glad to recommend it.

—Tim Challies, author, *Seasons of Sorrow*

I'm so grateful for this resource! In a world of subjective spirituality,
my friend Costi Hinn offers rock-solid biblical guidance for discerning God's will. This book replaces confusion with clarity, anxiety
with confidence, and mysticism with biblical methodology. Through
a careful handling of Scripture and practical wisdom, Costi provides
a framework for decision-making that honors God (which is all that
matters). This is more than just a book about finding God's will, it's
a pastoral and practical guide for a lifetime of faithful choices. A true
gift to the church.

—Jonny Ardavanis, pastor, Stonebridge Bible
Church; author, *Consider the Lilies*

Walking in God's Will is a practical guide to understanding and
implementing the will of God. This book helps simplify a topic we
often overcomplicate by encouraging us to view decision-making as a

spiritual discipline. Costi prioritizes our need to approach this topic with a humble heart and focus on our obedience to and confidence in the Word of God.

—Brianna Harris, dean of women, The Master's University

This book is a wonderfully clear, short, and persuasive guide for anyone wrestling with God's will in ordinary and trying circumstances. I love that this book drips with the Bible and that it has a subtle subtext of missions woven throughout the stories and chosen Scriptures. Followers of Christ will find this a helpful resource, but it will be beneficial for those who are new and growing in the grace of our God.

—Brooks Buser, president, Radius International

At some point in our lives, most of us have struggled with this question: "What does God want me to do next?" Decisions that impact family, church, relationships, and work, for example, shape the course of our lives; grappling with the significance of these decisions can often leave us feeling helpless, paralyzed, and unbelieving. Laying the foundation for godly and confident decision-making in the gospel, the Word of God, and the sovereign will of God, Costi Hinn provides practical and prudent counsel for believers in the crucible of difficult decision-making, gathering from Scripture (as well as personal experience) both general principles that apply to every believer and specific principles to guide in decision-making in real time. If you feel paralyzed in discerning the will of God for the next step in your life, this book—full of sound, pastoral advice—is perfect for you.

—Dr. Joel R. Beeke, chancellor and professor of systematic theology and homiletics, Puritan Reformed Theological Seminary

If any pastor truly embodies the heart of a shepherd, it's Costi Hinn, and this book reflects that. Many Christians often wrestle with how to discern God's will, myself included. After reading this book, I felt a renewed conviction and deep encouragement. I immediately wanted to go pick up my Bible and read it. Practical and rich with Scripture, *Walking in God's Will* guides us to understand that walking in God's will is ultimately about loving God, loving others, and living in alignment with His Word.

—Melissa Dougherty, popular YouTuber; author, *Happy Lies*

WALKING
in GOD'S
WILL

OTHER BOOKS BY COSTI W. HINN

God, Greed, and the (Prosperity) Gospel:
How Truth Overwhelms a Life Built on Lies

More Than a Healer: Not the Jesus
You Want, but the Jesus You Need

Knowing the Spirit: Who He Is, What He Does,
and How He Can Transform Your Christian Life

WALKING
in GOD'S
WILL

Demystify God's Plan for Your Life
and Make Decisions with Confidence

COSTI W. HINN

ZONDERVAN
BOOKS

ZONDERVAN BOOKS

Walking in God's Will
Copyright © 2025 by Costi W. Hinn

Published in Grand Rapids, Michigan, by Zondervan. Zondervan is a registered trademark of The Zondervan Corporation, L.L.C., a wholly owned subsidiary of HarperCollins Christian Publishing, Inc.

Requests for information should be addressed to customercare@harpercollins.com.

Zondervan titles may be purchased in bulk for educational, business, fundraising, or sales promotional use. For information, please email SpecialMarkets@Zondervan.com.

ISBN 978-0-310-36685-0 (audio)

Library of Congress Cataloging-in-Publication Data

Names: Hinn, Costi W. author.
Title: Walking in God's will : demystify God's plan for your life and make decisions with confidence / Costi W. Hinn.
Description: Grand Rapids, Michigan : Zondervan Books, [2025]
Identifiers: LCCN 2024046670 (print) | LCCN 2024046671 (ebook) | ISBN 9780310366805 (trade paperback) | ISBN 9780310366843 (ebook)
Subjects: LCSH: God (Christianity)—Will. | Christian life—Evangelical authors. | BISAC: RELIGION / Christian Living / Calling & Vocation | RELIGION / Faith
Classification: LCC BV4509.5 .H555 2025 (print) | LCC BV4509.5 (ebook) | DDC 248.4—dc23/eng/20241115
LC record available at https://lccn.loc.gov/2024046670
LC ebook record available at https://lccn.loc.gov/2024046671

Published in association with the literary agency of Wolgemuth & Associates, Inc.

Cover design: Studio Gearbox
Cover illustrations: Picksell / Shutterstock; Prixel Creative / Lighthouse
Interior design: Sara Colley

Printed in the United States of America

24 25 26 27 28 LBC 5 4 3 2 1

To Brett McIntosh,
my co-laborer in the local church,
who shows up early, stays late, and moved his family to Arizona
with no guarantees that our church plant would work.
I am thankful that the Lord willed what we always wished for.
It's a joy to serve Christ alongside such a faithful friend.

CONTENTS

ACKNOWLEDGMENTS

One afternoon I walked into the office of my fellow pastor and friend Brett McIntosh. He was meeting with a member involved with the prayer ministry at Shepherd's House. I apologized for interrupting their meeting and said, "Quick question for you brothers: If you had to pick between two book topics [I told them which ones], which would you say is a bigger need right now?" Both immediately responded, "A book on God's will!" Considering the men were involved with major segments of our church ministry, who better to ask for insight on the kinds of questions people have? They settled it for me, and for that I am grateful.

For this and every other book I write, my wife, Christyne, deserves gratitude and recognition. In what has been our busiest year to date on all fronts, including our marriage, family, local church, For the Gospel, ministry travel, and my doctorate, her faithfulness, support, and encouragement have been off the charts, not to mention her late-night lattes for my long writing sessions, her home-cooked meals, and her wisdom. Nobody takes care of me like my wife. I could not do this without her.

Our church family at Shepherd's House, including our elders, deacons, and staff, have been incredibly supportive of my writing and in providing resources that edify the church. Seeing the way our team shares the load of ministry with joy is evidence of the unity, love, and genuine friendship the Lord has seen fit to provide us. I love you all and pray that books like this are a blessing to you.

I'm also grateful to my team at For the Gospel who have continued to ensure that we provide sound doctrine for everyday people. Everything we do is made possible in large part by our Gospel Patrons, who graciously and generously support our ministry so that people can have access to free resources in more than 180 countries.

Finally, to Erik Wolgemuth and the team at Zondervan, I am grateful that we can all partner together to publish books that glorify God and strengthen his people. What a fulfilling and joyful purpose that is!

Introduction

GOD, WHAT SHOULD I DO?

Arizona, Here We Come!

Just before the panic of 2020 unraveled churches, communities, cities, friendships, and, of course, the economy, my wife and I sat in the living room on a gorgeous California spring day discussing the future. We had no idea what it might hold. But before us was one of the biggest and most difficult decisions we'd ever made as a married couple. Should we move to Arizona or Texas, or stay in California?

I had received job offers from two churches and had my current role to consider. Which church should we work with? What role should I take? Where would we raise our kids? How might things turn out? Whom could we trust? I really wished God would just write the decision on our wall, like that

1

time in Daniel 5:5–12 when a hand materialized at the feast of Belshazzar, but not even a paint chip appeared on our drywall.

I had been working at our church for nearly seven years, serving as the youth pastor, the family-life pastor, the adult-ministries pastor, and the executive pastor, all while completing my seminary studies. Each role was exciting as we built infrastructure, raised up leaders, and equipped the body, but after saying yes to the executive-pastor role, I was withering. I'd accepted the role because I wanted to be a team player, but it meant having little time to study and preach the Word and spending lots of time staring at spreadsheets, dealing with administrative support, and doing anything the senior pastor didn't want to do.

I loved the people, but deep down I knew I was not fulfilling my purpose, not because I didn't like the mundane parts of ministry, but because such a low percentage of my role matched my gifts and desire to shepherd, study, preach, and lead. But what could I do? I had no opportunities and knew that being faithful was the only option. To make matters more frustrating, I would get invited every few months to preach somewhere other than my home church and would spend two to three days there teaching, fellowshiping, and being with people in the trenches of their ministry, and then it was back to the spreadsheets, senior-pastor to-do list, and limited time to study.

During this very frustrating season of ministry, I felt like a mercenary with a dirty secret. Sometimes I would sulk, thinking, *Everywhere I travel, I am seen as a Bible-teaching pastor, a people person, a shepherd, and a teacher who is ful-filling his purpose. Where I actually work, though, I am a spreadsheet-tinkering, agenda-printing, logistics-handling fraud who spends his time dreaming not about all of that stuff but about growing old as a shepherd who is studying, preach-ing, writing, counseling, training men, guiding members, and bonding with his fellow elders and deacons.*

That's extreme, I know, but it's how I felt. While any staff pastor has to perform mundane tasks, I wanted to spend more time pastoring. That was my will. But would it ever be God's will? I had been asking God to open doors for more than a year, but he wasn't doing it.

On the home front, we had three young children. Our youngest was in diapers, our next oldest was in pull-ups, and our firstborn was just settling into his fourth different apart-ment or condo in six years as we frequently had to move into cheaper housing to afford to live until a family from another church let us rent their condo for way under market. It wasn't a perfect life, but it was *our* life. The last thing I wanted to do was let my goals lead my family down a dead-end road or to disobey God's will by pursuing my own will. You probably know the feeling.

Then, from what seemed like out of nowhere, the job opportunities came knocking. The first was as a discipleship pastor at a growing Bible church in Arizona whose average attendance was five to six hundred people, where I would be establishing ministries and preaching weekly to about twenty or more high school students. The second was as a young-adults pastor at a megachurch in Texas that averaged some fifteen thousand, where I would be preaching weekly to thousands of college students and young adults.

Every time I thought about the fork in the road we'd come to, pros and cons came to mind. Should we go? Should we stay?

In the end, we went to Arizona.

If you've read the bio on the cover of this book, you know that we've put down deep roots in the desert. I pastor a church in Chandler, Arizona, which we planted in 2022 after serving for three years at the Bible church that recruited me away from California. During the church-planting process, everything went wildly right. That Bible church and my pastor friends there kept every promise, made their intentions clear, and supported our plant.

Looking back on the past five years, it seems like it wasn't just the right decision, it was the only decision I can imagine having made. Hindsight is twenty-twenty. If we'd stayed in California, I would have been miserably unfulfilled. The church there ended up going through a relocation related to COVID that required a real executive pastor (not a fake one like me) who could devote seventy hours a week to finding a building and establishing a corporate structure. My lack of skill would have been a barrier to their goals. Going to Texas would have been a nightmare because the pastor who offered me the job ended up publicly stepping down a very short time later, and I would have been philosophically out of touch with that church's approach to megachurch ministry.

When I look back, I don't see a trivial decision that gently registered on the Richter scale of our future. Instead, I see a decision that was like a 9.5-magnitude earthquake under an ocean, triggering a tidal wave that we're still riding. We now have six kids, three born here in Arizona. We have forged new and life-altering friendships, seen old friends reenter our lives, and experienced God connect us to a church that is growing and thriving.

But guess what? We didn't know any of that would happen any more than we know how the next five years will go. What if trials come that are "Arizona specific" and someone says, "That never would have happened had you stayed in California"? What if someone we love dies? How steady will the ship be on the stormy days that are inevitable for churches, relationships, and other aspects of our lives?

The obvious answer is that all of these potential trials happen no matter where we are, because the Bible tells us trials are a matter of not "if" but "when" (James 1:2–4). Thinking about mishaps and trying to predict every outcome can be a lot like a blackjack gambler agonizing over whether he should hit or stay, or like a stock trader sweating over whether to sell as a stock sinks or soars.

That uncertainty is why the question of how to know God's will is a timeless one for Christians and undoubtedly something we all wrestle with, because our lives depend on it. I've written this book because, in the midst of that uncertainty, God has given us a way to build confidence.

The End of FOMO

One of the terms I've heard frequently among college students is *FOMO*, which stands for "fear of missing out." You get FOMO when you aren't at an event, but everyone is posting about it on social media. You get FOMO when your friends are hanging out but didn't invite you. You get FOMO when you believe the highlight reels on social media reflect how people are really living. Could there be a better way to describe the feeling that far too many Christians experience when it comes to God's will? We are crippled and crushed because we are insecure about knowing the will of God. We second-guess ourselves and become dizzy with retroactive remorse, wondering, *What if we had stayed instead? What if we had decided to go instead of stay? If we had made that decision, we would be better off.*

We see other people living the dream, walking in the blessings of God (spiritually and materially), making decisions, moving to new places, starting businesses, thriving in ministry, enjoying their marriages, and bonding with children and grandchildren, and we think, *I have missed God's will! My life will never be what it could have been.*

This Is a Battle You Can Win

If you often wonder, "God, what should I do?" and if knowing God's will seems more like a hard-fought battle than smooth sailing, then this book will provide you with two encouragements: (1) You're normal! And (2) God has provided the knowledge you need to make decisions with confidence and to trust him with the unknowns. Whether or not you believe these truths yet, you need to be aware that Satan lies to erode your confidence in God. He is 100 percent against your discovering God's will, because nothing destroys his plans more than people walking in the truth. Here are some of his favorite lies: comparison, callousness, and complacency.

Comparison

Comparison is defined as a consideration or estimate of the similarities or dissimilarities between two things or people. Satan doesn't care whether comparison causes us to copy others (trying to be similar) or to cower in fear (trying to be dissimilar), as long as he can get us to shift our eyes from God's will to focus on everybody else. For some of us, it's all about getting us to copy other people and abandon our calling and purpose in the Lord. We love their lives and want something similar, so we abandon the path God has us on. Satan wants us to chase that new location, that new house, that new style, or that big purchase to keep up with the Joneses— not for the right reasons. They say comparison is the thief of joy. Why? Because it robs us of contentment. Nothing leads us into frustration and disappointment more than allowing the will and whims of others to drive our decisions.

For others of us, comparison that gets us to cower in fear is about getting us to look at how things turned out for someone else. We want to be as dissimilar as possible, seeing how their life ended up because they followed Jesus, and go in a different direction! Imagine that every missionary in history looked at their persecuted predecessors and then, because of comparison and a desire to avoid that, cowered in fear. What if would-be church leaders looked at how pastors go through challenges and thought, "I am not running into the ministry, I am running from the ministry!" What if another family's difficult experience of job relocation makes you question God's call for *you* to make a professional change?

Satan wants us to superstitiously use the challenges of others as a predictor of outcomes for our lives. He doesn't care how we do it, so long as we operate on man's ideas instead of God's.

Callousness

Satan loves to lure us into a posture of callousness toward God's will. He wants us to embrace sentiments like "Who cares? I never seem to get it right when it comes to making decisions" and attitudes like "God didn't work things the way I wanted them to go last time, so I am going to do things my way this time around." In these frames of mind, we miss out on God's purposes for our lives because we've grown embittered and indifferent.

Complacency

Perhaps Satan's lulling us into complacency is the subtlest of his lies. It goes like this: Life is fine as it is. There's no need to rock the boat with decisions. If we take this next step of faith or go out on a limb, we'll just be disappointed or, worse, we could make a mess of things. If it ain't broke, don't fix it!

I can't tell you how many people I counsel or talk to say complacency is their number one problem when it comes to knowing and living out God's will. They're insecure or (buckle up here!) lazy because their lives are on cruise control. The hard truth is we all can be lazy at times, and while we may talk about how elusive God's will seems to be, we can be quite content to do nothing to find out what it is. We have to resist the Enemy's invitation to stagnation. The more we know, the more accountable we are for living out what we know. Complacency masquerades as easy comfort and freedom, but make no mistake, it's a detour from the destination.

The Number One Quality Needed to Walk in God's Will

We need one key quality more than any other for exploring God's will. This virtue is required to embrace Scripture and to win the wrestling match that often happens in our hearts with God's will. This quality is humility.

The essence of Christian humility is captured in Romans 12:3, where Paul the apostle writes, "For by the grace given to me I say to everyone among you not to think of himself more highly than he ought to think, but to think with sober judgment, each according to the measure of faith that God has assigned" (ESV).

This verse comes in the context of the topic of spiritual gifts. We are all a part of the body of Christ, all used by God for his purposes, and we all need to remember that we are not the center of everything. Why is that truth helpful when we study the topic of God's will? Because we sometimes cross-examine God as though he were a witness in a courtroom and must answer to us. When we seek God's will, we need to be careful that, deep down, we aren't just trying to figure out how to get our own will. We need humility to live out our purpose as Christians.

We see this warning throughout Scripture. In Romans 9:20, Paul warns us to be careful of pridefully presuming that we know God's purposes for everything he allows or does: "But who are you, O man, to answer back to God?" (ESV). In chapters 38–40 of Job, we find some of the most eye-opening views of God's character. After Job hits a low point and basically argues that he is righteous and doesn't deserve the suffering God has allowed, God responds by saying, "Who is this that darkens counsel by words without knowledge?" He then goes on to say, "I will ask you, and you instruct Me! Where were you when I laid the foundation of the earth?" (38:2–4 NASB 1995).

It's one of the most humbling moments in Scripture. God challenges someone who thinks he knows better than the Almighty. (We're guilty of this too!) Job eventually responds by saying, "Behold, I am insignificant; what can

I say in response to You?" (40:4). The picture we get is not of a mean and insensitive God who doesn't care about our questions. On the contrary! The idea is that we *can* express ourselves to God and seek answers, but we must be careful not to indict him or alter theological truths to satisfy our prideful opinions or lower him to a puppet who answers to us as puppeteers.

We must maintain reverence when considering his will. We must be in awe of his sovereign power when considering his purposes. We must also be in awe of his lovingkindness and tender mercy, because he most certainly understands our struggle to comprehend his will. In all of these things, we must be humble.

Five Words to Guide the Journey

When reading a book, as when going on a road trip, knowing where we're going reduces anxiety and elevates excitement. With that in mind, I want to convey my goals for you and provide some guidance on how to approach this book so you'll have a road map for the journey ahead. The following five words will help you understand my vision.

1. Practical

This book is practical. To begin, I want to meet you where you are and help you see that you're normal in your desire to walk in God's will. It's 100 percent normal to want to get decisions right, to aim for the best scenario, and to want to please God. In light of this, the very first chapter provides an answer to the question, "What is God's will for my life?" I want to bring the cookies down from the top shelf right away!

From there, we'll keep exploring God's will, finding more layers that help us form a strong foundation for our lives. In each chapter, we'll end with a practical summary called "Learning to Live," where you'll find questions to help you lead a small group discussion or engage in personal reflection.

2. Biblical

This book is biblical. Certain elements make some books more enjoyable than others, such as practical lists, personal stories, examples, applications, and principles. But above all else, a book needs to be biblical to have any use for us as Christians. So I've made it my goal to give you lots of Scripture in these pages. The most important truth is not what Costi says but what the Bible says. As you navigate each chapter, you'll get plenty of biblical truth to guide your decision-making.

3. Theological

This book is theological. It will fail to achieve its purpose if it doesn't provide major theological answers to questions about God's will. Theology matters, and even if you don't totally agree with my positions, you will be stronger than ever if you simply wrestle with them. Of course, I won't be able to cover every theological debate on this topic (they can be endless), but I will endeavor to cover the key ones.

4. Personal

This book is personal. I've never been mysterious in my writing and preaching ministries, nor do I treasure that quality in leaders. If someone is going to preach to me, lead me, write a book for me, instruct me, I want to know them, see them, and gain insight into their life. I don't trust a person who only "tells" but doesn't "show." When Paul calls the Corinthians to "be imitators of me, just as I also am of Christ" (1 Cor. 11:1), he has already shared with them his life, his heart, and his experience. I see his example as admirable and commendable. So in this book I share stories from my own decision-making process and experiences that serve not as "chapter and verse" commands for you to follow but rather as relatable examples of how one might apply biblical principles. As you sift through all of the material in this book, you might consider using this action grid:

What Costi shared that is biblical = *Do it*
What Costi shared that helps me think about our
 situation = *Consider it*
What Costi did that I would do differently in our
 context = *Customize it*
What Costi did that doesn't apply to my situation yet
 = *File it*

My convictions are never your commands. I simply hope that some aspect of my own decision-making can encourage you to know that you're not alone in the struggle of walking in God's will.

5. Counterintuitive

This book is counterintuitive. One of the key chapters in the book is titled "Your View of God's Word Shapes Your View of God's Will." The way I come at this chapter is pure, unadulterated bibliology (the study of the doctrine of Scripture). It's perhaps the most unlikely chapter in a book on God's will, but I'm taking a counterintuitive approach. I believe that if you have a strong foundation in bibliology, then you will trust the Bible more than you do emotions, peer pressure, doubts, fears, and anything else.

This chapter on Scripture is like a level for a builder who is framing a home. (You are the home builder.) A level might not be your primary tool for hammering a nail into your frames, but without it, your frames will be crooked!

In addition to that chapter, you will find other counterintuitive insights that invite you away from today's culture—which sometimes models quick reactions, emotional responses, and knee-jerk decisions—and toward thoughtful, prudent, wise decision-making.

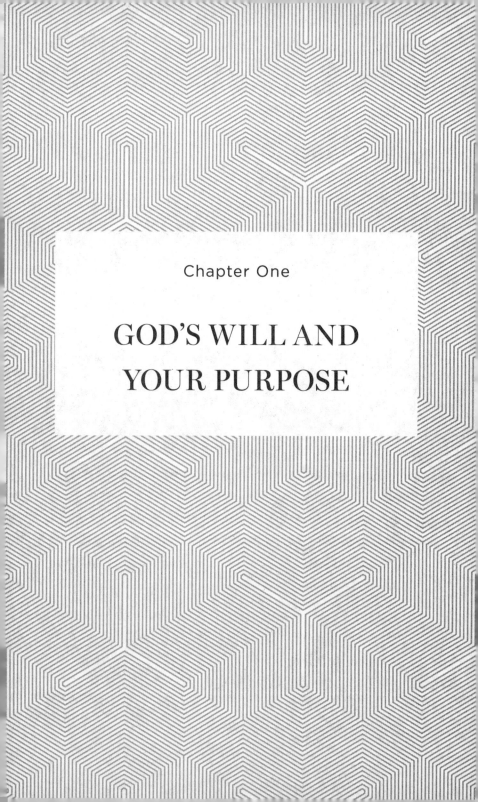

Chapter One

GOD'S WILL AND YOUR PURPOSE

Since I was a kid, I have always loved big working dogs. Common working dog breeds include bullmastiff, German shepherd, Great Dane, boxer, cane corso, and Siberian husky. After high school I got a dog of my very own, a best friend that changed my life—a Dogue de Bordeaux, or French bullmastiff. His name was Muscle (or, more formally, Mr. Muscle), and for good reason. He was a good boy, and quite a gentleman, but he was a *big* boy, built like a cinder block. While still a puppy at heart, he tipped the scales at 125 pounds when he was fully grown.

As I explored the purchase of a dog that could easily break through a sliding glass door, the man who sold the dog to me invited me over to meet his other mastiffs and teach me about working breeds. He was adamant that I grasp an important point if I wanted to keep Mr. Muscle safe and healthy—and my home undamaged.

He taught me that working dogs need purpose, clarity, discipline, focus, consistency, and communication. *Whoa!* I remember thinking. *This dog is not a yard ornament or just a cute house pet. He needs a purpose or he can become his own worst enemy.* As I further researched working dog breeds, I learned that dogs without a purpose can end up falling into any number of negative behaviors, including aggression. Without a purpose to channel their energy, they are more likely to tear up the house, chew through couches, or even attack their owners.

Like these working dog breeds, we need purpose too.

God designed us for purpose. Many of our problems are the result of either getting off the path of our purpose or having little purpose. We can be our own worst enemies when we live without aim. God's will is a lifeline that pulls us out of the chaos of purposeless existence.

In the beginning, when God created the world, he capped the beauty and glory of creation by making Adam and Eve in his image and then giving them a purpose. Genesis 1:26–28 says:

> Then God said, "Let Us make man in Our image, accord-ing to Our likeness; and let them rule over the fish of the sea and over the birds of the sky and over the cattle and over all the earth, and over every creeping thing that creeps on the earth." God created man in His own image, in the image of God He created him; male and female He created them. God blessed them; and God said to them, "Be fruitful and multiply, and fill the earth, and subdue it; and rule over the fish of the sea and over the birds of the sky and over every living thing that moves on the earth." (NASB 1995)

Consider the call to Adam and Eve to live fruitfully and productively, and to have influence over the earth by way of both procreation and administration. God did not make man-kind and send them on a never-ending vacation but instead put them in a paradise and told them to thrive and live with purpose. Adam was called to "cultivate" the garden and "keep it," which carries the idea of watching over it (Genesis 2:15 NASB 1995). God gave Adam not a temporary job but an ongoing purpose. Have you ever considered the way God delegated purpose to Adam to such a degree that he brought Adam the animals and let him decide what to call them? What a résumé builder! First employer? God. First job? Naming God's creation!

Even after the fall and the entrance of sin into the world, certain things did not change. Marriage didn't change (though we now deal with the curse of sin), God's love for people made in his image didn't change, and God's intention for his people to live with purpose didn't change. Though all things move toward redemption, accomplished by Christ on the cross, and we look forward to his glorious return, we don't find any support in Scripture for a "just sit around and wait for Jesus" approach to life.

The narrative of Genesis—and the rest of Scripture— shouts that humanity was made with purpose, for purpose. If we want to understand what it means to walk in God's will, we must begin with understanding that he has willed purpose for his people from the very beginning. You were never meant to coast through life on cruise control. You were never meant to sit around wondering whether you matter or whether your life has any significance. God breathed life into your lungs so that you would use your life for his purpose. Life and time are treasures given to you as gifts. Like all gifts, they are meant to be used to the fullest. The question is this: Are you using your time to live life on purpose?

In this chapter I want you to see that no matter what questions swirl in your mind regarding God's will and what the future may hold, you can experience greater fulfillment knowing you are in God's will by redeeming the time you've been given.

Your View of Time Affects How You Live Your Purpose

Vince Lombardi was a football coach who was so legendary that the NFL named the Super Bowl trophy after him when he died in 1970. Lombardi famously said of the Green Bay Packers, the team he coached for nine seasons and led to win five championships: "The Green Bay Packers never lost a game, we just ran out of time." In sports, as in life, there is a clock ticking down second by second, but unlike in sports, you cannot stop the clock of life. There are no time-outs, no halftime, intermissions, or overtime. You can't stop the clock for injury, and you can't finish the play you started before the clock strikes zero.

Life is like an hourglass through which the sands of time are falling, even in this moment. And isn't that what makes time so precious? Because it's slipping away.

But God has given us agency to use our time as best we can.

In his letter to the Ephesians, Paul was helping Christians live their faith boldly and purposefully. In Ephesians 5:15–17 we find some of the most practical truths of the entire letter. Digging into these truths will empower you to know how to make the most of time.

1. Be a Focused Christian

In Ephesians 5:15, Paul writes, "So then, be careful how you walk." By this point in his letter, the Ephesians have the idea fresh in their minds of being imitators of God (Eph. 5:1), being "light" (5:8), and living for Christ in a dark world. They know the truth (the "what"), and now he tells them to live that truth (the "how"). Paul's instruction to them is what we all need to remember: to live as light in this dark world we need to be focused, thoughtful, and intentional about the way we live. This is a major part of God's will for us.

"Be careful how you walk" means taking a close look at your decisions. It is God's will that Christians consider the weight of life and get serious about their purpose. We are called to stay focused on why we're here. Francis Foulkes says the phrase translates to "Be strictly careful then about the life you lead."[1] The King James Bible uses the word "circumspectly," which comes from two Latin words that together mean "to look around."

There is an exactness in how we're called to live our lives. Being exact doesn't mean making perfect decisions. Being exact means being intentional about purpose. Think of this life as a minefield full of dangers and distractions that can destroy you in an instant, but with care, focus, and intentionality you can walk through it with confidence. Being "careful" in the way you walk is much different from being "fearful" in the way you walk. The point of Ephesians 5:15–17 is that if you make the most of your time, and you are wise, and you know what the will of God is, then it's going to be a great ride, even when the road gets bumpy.

In a conversation about walking carefully and redeeming time, a churchgoer once said to me, "It sounds kind of limiting and uptight to be constantly mindful about all of this. Jesus died for me, I know I'm forgiven, and he's won victory. Why can't I just live my life and enjoy it without worrying and getting all serious about the details?" I appreciated the candor but also took note of the false binary crippling this beloved friend. My friend assumed that there are only two options: either you get to have fun and live without worrying about getting serious about life (winner!), or you get serious about the way you live but it's spiritually oppressive and boring (loser!). With a big smile on my face, I told this friend, "Excuse me? Paul would like a word!" And we went to 1 Corinthians 9.

In 1 Corinthians 9, Paul is explaining to the Corinthians that they have Christian freedom to do all sorts of things and can have a wonderful time enjoying life and liberty. But in the midst of their liberties and enjoyment of life, they are still called to think carefully about the way they live and what they're living for. At the beginning of the chapter, Paul says, "Am I not free? Am I not an apostle? Have I not seen Jesus our Lord? Are you not my work in the Lord?" (v. 1).

He is free to do many things. But by choice he elects to

stay balanced, focused, and mindful of the way he's living and relating to the world around him. Why? Because he knows to whom he belongs. Talk about purpose—what an example we have in Paul. Let's walk through the passage verse by verse and notice the theme that emerges.

Paul writes, "I do all things for the sake of the gospel, so that I may become a fellow partaker of it" (1 Cor. 9:23). Paul was supporting himself financially by making tents. He could have taken a paycheck from the churches but chose not to. Instead, he used his tent-making income to support his ministry. He worked hard to relate with people however he could and to reach whomever he could for the sake of the gospel.

"Do you not know that those who run in a race all run, but *only* one receives the prize? Run in such a way that you may win" (v. 24). What is the point of running the race of life unless you're winning? To Paul, "winning" was making a huge deal about Christ!

"Everyone who competes in the games exercises self-control in all things. So they do it to obtain a perishable wreath, but we an imperishable" (v. 25). Winners are disciplined and self-controlled. They are focused. They go about their business in a certain way and get out what they put in. If they work hard the right way, they win the reward, but that reward is still perishable. A believer who runs the race of life the right way sees not only earthly results, which eventually fade, but eternal rewards that last forever.

"Therefore I run in such a way as not to run aimlessly;

WALKING in GOD'S WILL

I box in such a way, as to avoid hitting air, but I strictly discipline my body and make it my slave, so that, after I have preached to others, I myself will not be disqualified" (vv. 26–27). Paul is saying he wants to run toward a target with self-control, self-denial, and focus. He wants to achieve his life goal of glorifying God through spreading the gospel.

Paul's words to the Corinthians parallel his words to the Ephesians about walking carefully. Being saved by Christ leads to living intentionally for Christ. Unfortunately today, just as in the early church, many Christians are sleepwalking. We have become spiritual drifters floating down a lazy river. Perhaps that's where every discussion of God's will begins. We each have to ask, *What is my purpose?* Then and only then can we begin to understand God's will and how to live it.

My friend, don't sleep on this life you've been given. Focus on why you are here, why you have the gifts you have, and what you're doing for the glory of God and the gospel. Take inventory of all areas of your life. Enjoy creation, rejoice in God's good gifts, laugh, and make memories. And remember that all of these things interweave with your larger purpose. How are you managing what God has given you, and how does it fit into his purpose for you?

"A weakness of all human beings is trying to do too many things at once," said Henry Ford. "That scatters effort and destroys direction. It makes for haste, and haste makes waste." This is where focus begins for the Christian. The secret to success for a lion seeking to take down a zebra on the savanna is to pick one target out of the herd of hundreds. The lion doesn't chase all the zebras—he chases one. If you're going to achieve the purpose of your life as a believer, you need to lock onto the target of living for Christ.

Following God's will means walking carefully and focusing on your purpose, which is why Paul makes the next point.

2. Be a Wise Christian

Paul continues in Ephesians 5:15 by saying we should walk "not as unwise people but as wise." The Greek word *asophos* means "foolish," and *sophos* means "intelligent." These words are separated by only one letter, and doesn't it make a world of difference? Some people build their lives wisely, and some build their lives foolishly. Wisdom is one of the most treasured assets you can acquire as a believer, and it begins with the fear of the Lord. In contrast, the fool walks through life like a captain who has set sail on a ship but has not charted the course. Many in this world find living in a fool's paradise to be great fun until the rent is due. So it is with life. God's will calls us to live wisely.

In Luke 12:16–21, Jesus tells a parable, saying,

"The land of a rich man was very productive. And he began thinking to himself, saying, 'What shall I do, since I have no place to store my crops?' And he said, 'This is what I will do: I will tear down my barns and build larger ones, and I will store all my grain and my goods there. And I will say to myself, "You have many goods stored up for many years to come; relax, eat, drink, and enjoy yourself!'" But God said to him, 'You fool! This very night your soul is demanded of you; and as for all that you have prepared, who will own it now?' Such is the one who stores up treasure for himself, and is not rich in relation to God."

The point of the parable is that we miss the purpose of our lives if all we do is accumulate wealth and build our own little kingdoms. If we've lived only for ourselves, even if we've lived it up, we've not truly lived as God intended. What a piercing question God asks in the parable: "And as for all that you have prepared, who will own it now?" If we spend our lives trying to be wealthy and neglecting spiritual priorities, we will gain nothing. As Christians we are called to ask ourselves, *How can I build God's kingdom?* not *How can I build bigger barns?*

Jesus' parable helps us appreciate Paul's words in Ephesians 5:17 all the more when he says, "Do not be foolish, but understand what the will of the Lord is." What God wants us to do with our lives is not a secret. As Paul writes to the Ephesians, it's God's will that we should live out his commands. And Paul says don't be foolish, because only a fool would ignore a treasure sitting before him.

Here are five illustrations from the book of Proverbs that show the contrast between the fool and the wise person. Each of these will have an impact on how you discover God's will and make decisions in life.

1. **The wise person values wisdom, the fool ignores it.**
   - Proverbs 1:7: "The fear of the LORD is the beginning of knowledge; fools despise wisdom and instruction."
   - Proverbs 9:8: "Do not rebuke a scoffer, or he will hate you; rebuke a wise person and he will love you."
   - **Takeaway:** We know the scoffers because they mock wisdom. The wise learn.
2. **The wise person knows riches are fleeting, the fool trusts in them.**
   - Proverbs 11:4: "Riches do not benefit on the day of wrath, but righteousness rescues from death."
   - Proverbs 11:28: "One who trusts in his riches will fall, but the righteous will flourish like the green leaf."
   - **Takeaway:** Money is a tool for providing for ourselves and may be a factor in major decisions, but it must not become the main driver for all our decisions in life. Money does us no good when our souls are in peril. Greed can easily lead us astray.
3. **The wise person works hard for what matters, the fool is lazy and pursues worthless things.**
   - Proverbs 12:11: "One who works his land will have plenty of bread, but one who pursues worthless things lacks sense."
   - **Takeaway:** You get out what you put in. What you chase you will catch, what you catch you can keep. So what are you working hard for? If you get what you want, do you have what matters most?

4. **The wise person takes inventory of his life, the fool is careless.**
   - Proverbs 27:23–24: "Know well the condition of your flocks, and pay attention to your herds. For riches are not forever, nor does a crown endure to all generations."
   - **Takeaway:** In every area of our lives—finances, time, friendships, romantic relationships, social media presence, work, goals—we would be wise to pay attention to the details and steward our assets well. The fool is careless, and his carelessness will catch up with him.

5. **The wise person makes decisions with knowledge, the fool acts without thinking.**
   - Proverbs 13:16: "Every prudent person acts with knowledge, but a fool displays foolishness."
   - Proverbs 22:3: "A prudent person sees evil and hides himself, but the naive proceed, and pay the penalty."
   - **Takeaway:** Wise people plan and execute their plans based on facts; a fool doesn't do this and displays his foolishness accordingly. Do we see someone's poor judgment leading down a road of evil? Is evil around us? We would be wise to distance ourselves from such things.

All of these truths apply to our lives and will save us from a world of trouble, but the most obvious contrast between the wise person and the fool is found in Psalm

14:1: "The fool has said in his heart, 'There is no God.'"
That's where foolishness finds its deep-seated root. To not
believe there is a God is to reject the foundational truth of
the universe, the human condition, and eternal life. But it is
just as dangerous to say that you believe in God while living
as though you don't.

Christians are called to live as salt and light in the world
(Matt. 5:13–16), and that is not disconnected from knowing
and walking in God's will. As Christians we are children of
God, and we are called to a higher purpose, to leverage all of
life for God's glory.

This leads us to the third way we can make the most of
our time.

3. Be a Productive Christian

In Ephesians 5:16, Paul emphasizes that his readers are
called to be "making the most of your time, because the
days are evil." "Making the most" literally means "to buy
up," and the idea here is to maximize time. There are two
words for time that Paul could have used in the original
Greek language he wrote in. *Chronos,* which is used for
exact time (e.g., 2:30 p.m.), and *kairos,* which can describe
a time period, such as the Dark Ages, one's childhood, or
the totality of one's life. We are called to be productive with
the time we've been given because the days are evil. This
world needs Jesus, and being a productive Christian means
knowing and living God's will so that we can be effective
with our purpose for his glory.

Do you know that feeling of satisfaction that comes from being productive? You were made to feel that every day for the sake of Christ and the gospel. You are hardwired to crave the joy of knowing something has eternal purpose. Productivity is rewarding, but being productive for God's purposes takes it to the next level. You will never know gospel-centered productivity until you know your purpose. Why are you here? Why were you saved? Why has God blessed you? Why are your eyes open? Why has he placed you in the place where you work, live, shop, study, and play? Are you buying up the time you've been given and maximizing it for the purposes of God?

Oswald Sanders once said, "Our problem is not too little time, but making better use of the time we have." Isn't that the truth?

Adoniram Judson is a beautiful example of this. He spent his existence on earth advancing the work of the gospel. He was the first American missionary to the people of Burma. He buried wives and children on the mission field. He wrote,

A life once spent is irrevocable. It will remain to be contemplated through eternity . . . . The same may be said of each day. When it is once past, it is gone forever. All the marks which we put upon it, it will exhibit forever. . . . Each day will not only be a witness of our conduct, but will affect our everlasting destiny. . . . How shall we then wish to see each day marked with usefulness . . . ! It is too late to mend the days that are past. The future is in our power. Let us, then, each morning, resolve to send the day into eternity in such a garb as we shall wish it to wear forever. And at night let us reflect that one more day is irrevocably gone, indelibly marked.[2]

You might not go to Burma (modern-day Myanmar) or die on the mission field, but you can view God's will and your life the way he did. You can resolve to spend each day on earth with eternity in mind and make your life count.

One of the greatest sermons I have ever heard on making life count was preached by John Piper. The words that particularly pierced my heart were these: "If you want your life to count, if you want the ripple effect of the pebbles you drop to become waves that reach the ends of the earth and roll on for centuries and into eternity, you don't have to have a high IQ or a high EQ. You don't have to have good looks or riches. You don't have to come from a fine family or a fine school. You just have to know a few great, majestic, unchanging, obvious, simple, glorious things, and be set on fire by them."[3]

The clock of life is running. Are you redeeming the time for the glory of God and the gospel? That's one of the key questions to ask as you seek to discern God's will.

Learning to Live

I believe that walking in God's will and making decisions with confidence is impossible without the power of the gospel at work in our lives. Why? Because the gospel is attached to our purpose, and the gospel transforms us. When we have placed our faith in Jesus Christ, we receive a brand-new heart (2 Cor. 5:17), and a new heart will supernaturally result in a new direction. As we reflect on our purpose and the way we approach decisions (with the wisdom of God versus in the foolishness of this world), living out the three truths below will be a game changer for our past, present, and future.

1. Repent of sin, turn to Christ in faith, and commit your life to God's glory. I like to say that no Christian ever graduates from the gospel. Can I encourage you to go back to the gospel again and again? You need it, I need it, and it takes us back to the foundational reality that we can do nothing apart from Christ (John 15:5). The gospel is a wellspring of living water to the parched soul. The gospel turns the bitter heart sweet with grace. The gospel melts the heart of stone into a soft and submissive vessel. You need the gospel to live out God's will.

There is no greater next step toward purpose than to turn from sin, put your faith in Jesus Christ, and commit to live for his glory. If you've never done that, today is the day of salvation—you can be born again and experience how Christ makes all things new. If you've been saved by his grace, go back to that first love that changed your life and renew your commitment to live for him all the more.

2. Focus on Christ as the key to your purpose. Identity is everything. Walking in the will of God starts with walking in your identity. Jesus doesn't save you and then say, "Okay, now you take it from here. Muster up the strength to be good enough, to stay saved, and get yourself to your destiny." Instead, the Bible reminds us that growth begins with our gaze. Where are you looking? If not on Christ, you won't make it.

Do you remember the story of Jesus walking on water and the lesson Peter learned in the process? Matthew 14:28–31 tells us: "Peter said to Him, 'Lord, if it is You, command me to come to You on the water.' And He said, 'Come!' And Peter got out of the boat, and walked on the water and came toward Jesus. But seeing the wind, he became frightened, and beginning to sink, he cried out, 'Lord, save me!' Immediately Jesus stretched out His hand and took hold of him, and said to him, 'You of little faith, why did you doubt?'" (NASB 1995).

Peter started out with his gaze fixed on Christ, even committing to do whatever the Lord asked. Before he knew it, he was walking on water! But the miracle was short-lived because Peter took his eyes off the one who called him out of the boat in the first place. He sank into the waves that the one who called him out of the boat controlled. How often do we fall into the same pattern? We're all in, only to take our eyes off the one who calls *and* sustains us. Purpose is found in Christ alone. Keep your gaze fixed on him.

3. Reject the worldly opinions of fools. With what Proverbs says about fools in mind, along with Paul's instruction to put away worldly patterns and walk in a manner worthy of your calling, you can confidently reject the opinions of those who live their lives for self-glory and self-satisfaction and boast that they are self-made. Instead, choose to heed and treasure the divine wisdom God provides for your purpose. There will be days when the Enemy will lie to you and put temptations in your path that invite you to take shortcuts, give up, or see God's will as little more than a cosmic killjoy meant to ruin the fun of life. The devil is predictable, having tempted Christ with the same self-serving routine, only to fail. He will fail with you as well if you stick to God's Word over his wicked lies. One of the primary ways he will assault you is through the peer-pressuring opinions of fools. Turn down the lies, turn up the truth.

Questions for Reflection and Discussion

1. Read Proverbs 12:11 and list potentially "worthless" pursuits that need to be either cut out of your life or reprioritized so that you are in a better position to live God's purpose for your life.
2. How have you seen purposelessness lead to destructive patterns in your life? Why is purpose so important for all people (and especially Christians)?
3. Why is the gospel essential to living out your purpose as a Christian?
4. What are some good things that can quickly become negative influences when they shift your eyes off Christ?

5. God's will for you is to redeem the time you have been given on this earth and live for his glory. How do you balance a Christ-focused and gospel-driven life without becoming legalistic over things such as fun, rest, and enjoyment of his good gifts?

Chapter Two

GOD'S WILL FOR EVERY CHRISTIAN

I once heard an old pastor tell a joke that always helps me appreciate the different ways that Christians process decisions and opportunities. The story goes that a pastor received a call from a church in another town that offered him a salary four times what he was being paid by his current church. Up to that point, the pastor was poorly treated and vastly underpaid, causing hardship to his family—and his wife bore the brunt of it. Ministering at this church had been a struggle for the pastor and his family, but he was determined to be faithful. He spent a great deal of time in prayer trying to discern what God wanted him to do. Then one day a family friend ran into the pastor's son in town and asked him which way his dad was leaning.

"Do you know what your dad is going to do?" the friend asked.

"Well," replied the son, "Dad's praying, but Mom's packing!"

Different People but the Same Principles

The truth is we're all different and we all process decisions differently. Yet there are certain truths that must remain the same—no matter how different we may be. In this chapter I'd like to give you a foolproof framework for walking in God's will no matter who you are, where you're from, or what your spiritual maturity is. I'll get into the practical aspects of decision-making and the theology of God's will along with some bibliology (the doctrine of Scripture). We will begin with the nonnegotiables that God desires for every Christian. Before focusing on personal goals and desires, a follower of Jesus commits to what God desires. Nobody should ever have to wonder, *What is God's will for me?*

As you reflect on this list, remember that these are not suggestions to be considered—they are commands to be obeyed. Does God care about what school you attend, which job you take, which house you buy, or whom you marry? Of course! But if you commit to embracing these ten aspects of God's will for your life, then no matter how your decisions turn out, you can have confidence knowing you are in God's will because you've followed what God's Word says. While these points may be my summation, they aren't *my* truth. Each one is rooted in Scripture.

The First Ten Steps to Walk in God's Will

1. Be Saved

Can you think of a better place to begin than with the heart-transforming, jaw-dropping, life-changing power of the gospel and salvation? I can't! If we're going to talk about walking in God's will, we must talk about the gospel. By "gospel" I mean the good news that Jesus Christ died to save sinners (1 Tim. 1:15), that when we were dead in our sins, God mercifully made us alive together with Christ, and that by grace we have been forgiven of our sins (Eph. 2:1–9). Instead of wrath and death as condemnation for our sin, we have been given freedom and life through Jesus (Rom. 6:23; 8:1). The truth is that we will never walk in God's will in the fullest and most joyful sense unless we are saved. Life without Christ is empty, even if we don't see that when we're blind in sin.

Out of all the steps I've outlined here, this one is the longest because it's the most important. Even for the longtime Christian who has heard the gospel thousands of times, we never graduate from the gospel. We need the gospel every day. Show me a Christian who thinks they have heard the gospel enough and I'll show you a Christian who needs to hear it again.

Being saved (I'll explain what that looks like in a minute) is the pinnacle of walking in God's will because it's the pinnacle of our purpose. Humanity was created for worship and relationship with our God and Creator. Throughout Scripture we see how God's will underpins our salvation. He is not an angry God who refuses to give sinners a second chance, nor is he a God who overlooks the need of sinners to be saved. So what does "being saved" look like?

First, being saved involves the repentance of sin according to God's will. The Greek word for "repentance" is *metanoia*, and it means "a change of mind." Repentance is not just regret for being caught in sin or having to suffer the consequences of sin; repentance is a change of mind about your decisions and the sin those decisions led to. Remorse is different from repentance because remorse is more about your feelings of guilt, but it does not necessarily mean you've changed your mind about your lifestyle, decisions, or sin.

For example, someone may feel remorse after being caught in adultery because of the consequences of their actions, but they make excuses to attempt to justify their behavior. Remorse causes people to feel bad about how others will view them. Remorse leads them to feel distress because they ruined their marriage and disappointed their children, but remorse does not lead to a change of mind.

Often people who are remorseful go back to their sinful behaviors once the emotions and turmoil of getting caught die down. Repentance, on the other hand, is a total change of mind, whether you are caught in your sin or not. Repentance is a piercing feeling in your heart that you have sinned against God and you no longer want to. Repentance is not merely the fear of being caught in sin, it is a hatred of your sin accompanied by a change of mind. The repentant person sees their sin in a new light and is resolved to fight it, hate it, and embrace the grace of God. The repentant person doesn't care about pleasing people but rather wants to please Jesus Christ.

One of the most powerful examples of repentance in the New Testament is when Jesus visits with a tax collector named Zacchaeus (Luke 19:1–10). In those days tax collectors were greedy cheaters. Everybody hated tax collectors because they stole money from hardworking people and the poor.

Zacchaeus had made himself wealthy by stealing from others and taking advantage of them. He was a corrupt sinner who deserved jail time and eventually hell. When Jesus visited with him, Zacchaeus exhibited genuine repentance, then gave away possessions to the poor, paid back those he had cheated, and even paid people more than he owed them (Luke 19:8).

The Corinthian church is another great example of repentance, and in their situation Paul refers to "the will of God" (2 Cor. 7:10). Paul had strongly rebuked the Corinthian church in his first letter to them, correcting many aspects of their church life and sinful behaviors. The book of 2 Corinthians shows us the response to his rebuke.

Did they run away? Did they respond in anger? Did they make excuses? No. They were so broken over their sin that Paul wrote to them again to say how proud he was of them for repenting as true followers of Jesus. Paul was sorry to have caused them such sorrow with his strong words, but he knew it was necessary and was overjoyed to see that they responded with humility and repentance. They felt godly sorrow, eagerness to clear themselves, indignation over their sin, and readiness to see justice done (2 Cor. 7:8–11).

King David is also an example we should reflect on. David wrote Psalm 51 after committing adultery with Bathsheba, having her husband murdered on the front lines, and brazenly using his position as king to cover up his sins. After being confronted by the prophet Nathan and experiencing the consequences of his sin (2 Sam. 12:1–24), David felt more than guilt over being caught—he was distraught over sinning against God. He declared, "A broken and a contrite heart, God, You will not despise" (Ps. 51:17).

Repentance is a key part of God's will because it is the motivation to seek Christ for salvation and forgiveness of sin.

Second, being saved involves faith in Jesus Christ and not in your own works. Ephesians 2:8–10 sheds light on the role of God's will in our salvation: "For by grace you have been saved through faith; and that not of yourselves, it is the gift of God; not as a result of works, so that no one may boast. For we are His workmanship, created in Christ Jesus for good works, which God prepared beforehand so that we would walk in them" (NASB 1995). In this gospel-rich passage we see that faith is essential to salvation and that salvation leads to our good works, which is precisely what God wills us to walk in. Do you see how being saved becomes imperative for walking in God's will? How can we live out our purpose if we do not come to faith in the one who has created us for purpose?

In 2 Peter 3:9, Peter says without apology, "The Lord is not slow about His promise, as some count slowness, but is patient toward you, not willing for any to perish, but for all to come to repentance." This not only causes us to say "Thank you!" to the Lord but also helps us answer the question "What does he want us to do?" He wants us to be saved, he wants us to place our faith in Jesus and repent of our sin, and he wants the saved people to share that message.

People worry so much about all kinds of decisions, saying, "God, what do you want me to do? Should I do this?

Or that?" I imagine that if God were to respond audibly, he might say, "My will is that people be saved. You don't even share the gospel in your own church or community, so why would you listen to any other direction I give you?" As one preacher often says, "If you can't say 'Amen!' you can at least say 'Ouch!'" How quick we are to seek the unique and adventurous aspects of God's will, wondering about the future and how we'll live out our dreams, when all along God is calling us into the simple act of obeying and sharing the gospel.

2. Be Different

At our church I like to remind people, "You were meant to be weird!" If you're a Christian, the world around you should look at you like you are a bit strange. I'm not talking about being reclusive, socially awkward, or obnoxious. I'm talking about your focus, your affections, your ethics, and the trajectory of your life. The Christian lives set apart from the world. This is so clear in Scripture that before we ask God for the juicy details about a job promotion and before we start scrolling Zillow for what gorgeous new house we hope is God's will for us, we should pause and take inventory of the way we are living our lives for Christ. You and I are called to be different. It is God's will that we are different!

What does this look like? Peter explains, "As obedient children, do not be conformed to the former lusts which were yours in your ignorance, but like the Holy One who called you, be holy yourselves also in all your behavior; because it is written, 'You shall be holy, for I am holy'" (1 Peter 1:14–16).

I find this to be one of the clearest passages about how Christians are to live when it comes to God's will. The idea of being holy is not so much about being perfect in the sense that you never sin or do anything wrong, but it is about being set apart, consecrated, and unlike the world when it comes to the way you do things.

There's an aspect to holiness that only God can possess. In theology holiness is considered one of God's incommunicable attributes; in other words, nobody can be holy like he is in his perfection. But it is also one of God's communicable attributes, because we are to imitate his being "other" or different.

When it comes to all of this "be different" talk, you might think I am being a bit intense and taking one little verse and stretching it too far, but I promise you, being different in every way is God's will for your life. When it comes to God's will and sanctification, sexual purity, sin, and submission to God, the Bible is loaded with explicit statements. Paul doesn't mince words in 1 Thessalonians 4:3 when he says, "For this is the will of God, your sanctification; that is, that you abstain from sexual immorality."

Have you ever thought about the implications of a verse like that? In the midst of our asking, "What should I do?" "Where should I move?" "Should I do this thing or that thing?" the will of God asks, "Are you as concerned with seeking freedom from pornography addiction or any other sexual sin as you are with making sure your material goals are being achieved? Are you praying about your holiness more than you're praying about your self-serving agenda?" We need this convicting reminder from God's Word. His will for us is sexual purity and our sanctification, and for us to live set-apart lives and be different in the way we deal with sin.

3. Be a Servant

As a follower of Jesus Christ, you are called to place your feet where he has placed his and to act as he did. There may be no more obvious a characteristic of Christ than his service to others. The Gospel of Matthew records the entire scene and also includes a vital lesson on being a servant that we would do well to take to heart. It is God's will that all followers of Jesus be a servant just as he was:

> Then the mother of the sons of Zebedee came to Jesus with her sons, bowing down and making a request of Him. And He said to her, "What do you wish?" She said to Him, "Command that in Your kingdom these two sons of mine may sit one on Your right and one on Your left." But Jesus answered, "You do not know what you are asking. Are you able to drink the cup that I am about to drink?" They said to Him, "We are able." He said to them, "My cup you shall drink; but to sit on My right and on My left, this is not Mine to give, but it is for those for whom it has been prepared by My Father."
>
> And hearing this, the ten became indignant with the two brothers. But Jesus called them to Himself and said, "You know that the rulers of the Gentiles lord it over them,

and their great men exercise authority over them. It is not this way among you, but whoever wishes to become great among you shall be your servant, and whoever wishes to be first among you shall be your slave; just as the Son of Man did not come to be served, but to serve, and to give His life a ransom for many."

—*Matthew 20:20–28 NASB 1995*

No matter what you pursue in your life as a Christian, consistent service to others is something God has called you to. Maybe you're in the midst of a season where you aren't sure what's next for your life, but you can be sure God wants you to serve while you wait on other doors to open. Maybe you're at a fork in the road with major decisions to pray about—well, one decision you never need to wonder about is whether you will serve. This could look like regular involvement within your local church during worship gatherings, but don't forget that worship isn't limited to Sundays. Worship is a lifestyle, and serving others is what we do every day.

Wherever God has put you, no matter how uncertain various factors may be, you can use your hands to be an extension of Christ. You can use your life to emulate his. That is always God's will for you. One of the great illustrations of God's will for us as servants is in the New Testament when Peter is writing to Christians who are in the midst of persecution. You might think a church leader would give people a break, considering all they've endured, but Peter intensifies his call, urging them to keep pressing forward. He writes in 1 Peter

4:10–11, "As each one has received a special gift, employ it in serving one another as good stewards of the manifold grace of God. Whoever speaks, is to do so as one who is speaking the utterances of God; whoever serves is to do so as one who is serving by the strength which God supplies; so that in all things God may be glorified through Jesus Christ, to whom belongs the glory and dominion forever and ever. Amen" (NASB 1995).

The simple truth is this: nobody is above serving others. Jesus, his disciples, the early church, the modern church, athletes, celebrities, business owners, pastors, and everybody in between. Labels lie and tell us we've earned top spot and are now to be served. Christ has called us to serve.

The life of D. L. Moody provides a nice example of the kind of serving Christ calls us to—no matter who we are. In the late 1800s a large group of European pastors came to one of Moody's Northfield Bible Conferences in Massachusetts. Following the European custom of the time, each guest put his shoes outside his room to be cleaned by the hall servants overnight. But this was America and there were no hall servants. Walking the dormitory halls that night, Moody saw the shoes and determined not to embarrass his brothers. He mentioned the need to some ministerial students who were there but was met with only silence or pious excuses not to help.

Moody returned to the dorm and gathered up the shoes, and, alone in his room, the world's most famous evangelist at that time cleaned and polished the shoes. Only the unexpected arrival of a friend in the midst of the work revealed the secret. When the foreign visitors opened their doors the next morning, their shoes were shined. They never knew by whom. Moody told no one, but his friend told a few people, and during the rest of the conference, different men volunteered to shine the shoes in secret.

Perhaps the episode provides some insight into why God used D. L. Moody as he did. He was a man with a servant's heart, and that was the basis of his greatness.[1]

4. Be Loving

In Luke 10:25–28 a lawyer asks Jesus the most important question anyone could ever ask. Luke records the moment: "And behold, a lawyer stood up and put him to the test, saying, 'Teacher, what shall I do to inherit eternal life?' And He said to him, 'What is written in the Law? How does it read to you?' And he answered, 'You shall love the Lord your God with all your heart, and with all your soul, and with all your strength, and with all your mind; and your neighbor as yourself.' And He said to him, 'You have answered correctly; do this and you will live.'"

What a transformation we would see in the church and in the world if Christians would pause their quests for selfish success and ask themselves, *Do I love God? Do I love others?* If I may be so bold, I would surmise that we typically come to the subject of God's will with our own wills in mind. If we were honest, we would admit that knowing God's will is so fascinating and interesting to us because we are interested in getting what we want out of God. It may be a little daunting to confess that, but it's healthy for us to expose our self-love, because from that place of honesty we begin to cultivate genuine love.

After that moment with the lawyer, Jesus goes on to tell the famous parable of the good Samaritan. In that parable a Jewish man is traveling from Jerusalem to Jericho when bandits rob him, beat him, strip him, and leave him half dead. A priest happens to walk by and, instead of helping, passes to the other side of the road. A Levite then follows, with the same response. But a Samaritan comes upon the man, and even though Samaritans and Jews were enemies and held animosity toward each other, the Bible says this particular Samaritan "felt compassion" for the beaten man (Luke 10:33).

He bound up the man's wounds and cared for him, then took him to an inn to recover—and he paid for his entire stay. Jesus tells all who are there that day, including the lawyer, that they are to go and do the same for others. His point is that his followers are called to both love God and love others. A life that walks in God's will is a life that walks in love.

John 13:34–35 records Jesus teaching, "A new commandment I give to you, that you love one another: just as I have loved you, you also are to love one another. By this all people will know that you are my disciples, if you have love for one another" (ESV). In all that you do, you are to love. In the pursuit of great things, you are to pursue the greatest thing, which is to love God and love others. One of the telltale signs that you have experienced salvation is that you are walking in the will of God to love. This means that you are led by what you know more than by what you feel. Elisabeth Elliot offers strong and helpful words about our emotions, exhorting us: "It is Christ who is to be exalted, not our feelings. We will know Him by obedience, not by emotions. Our love will be shown by obedience, not by how good we feel about God at a given moment. 'And love means following the commands of God.' 'Do you love Me?' Jesus asked Peter. 'Feed My lambs.' He was not asking, 'How do you feel about Me?' for love is not a feeling. He was asking for action."[2]

What we know is what our Lord, who loves us so much, would have us do. We are to love. This will mean forgiveness, tenderness, sacrifice, kindness, patience, peacemaking, and a host of other actions that come from the heart, because love always leads to action.

5. Be Generous

Over the past several years I've seen God provide for our gospel-focused ministries in jaw-dropping ways through the generosity of faithful Christians. I remember sitting with an individual who was generously giving to help us accomplish a vital project at For the Gospel. At the end of our discussion, I said, "Thank you for your generosity. I praise God for your willingness to get behind our effort." The response of my generous friend was, "Well, thank *you* for the opportunity. I praise God that we get to be a part of this."

I was struck by my friend's attitude that day, and it

opened my eyes to a perspective I had never considered before: *I shouldn't thank God just for the privilege of receiving. I should also thank God for the privilege of giving.* It's our joy to be a part of what God is doing. It's a joy for us to *get* to give. Instead of thinking of generosity as a burden or a drain on our resources, we can see it as a joyful opportunity.

Far too often we approach generosity with a limited mentality, not a liberal one. We wrongly think that God couldn't possibly give us more if we gave. Or we selfishly strategize: "More for them means less for me." Or we even forget what the Bible says about God owning the cattle on a thousand hills (Ps. 50:10), how he is the one who gives his people the ability to earn wealth (Deut. 8:18), and how Jesus modeled humility and consideration of others above ourselves (Phil. 2:3–7)— right down to giving his life for us.

When it comes to walking in God's will, the Christian does not seek to hold on but rather seeks to let go. The follower of Jesus makes it his or her goal to be a giver, not a keeper. I am of the conviction that God will close more doors on selfish Christians in order to wake them up from their disobedience and he will open more doors for generous Christians because he knows he has their hearts. About a decade ago I was still in the early years of being saved out of the prosperity gospel movement, and I had an extreme aversion to talking about money or even coming close to saying the sort of thing I just wrote here.

But after several years studying a biblical theology of stewardship, money, and generosity, I can say without a shred of doubt or insecurity that Christians, whether rich or poor, are called by God to be the most generous givers on planet Earth. Why? Because we have been created, loved, saved, favored, blessed, gifted, and deployed by God with such lavish grace that it would be the ultimate display of hypocrisy to not be generous in return. Generosity is not about the amount, it's about the heart. We are called to be copycats of the biggest Giver of all.

None of this is novel or my own idea. I'm borrowing this concept from both Jesus and the apostle Paul. When Paul was teaching the Corinthians about generosity in the book of 2 Corinthians, it was on the heels of having rebuked them with the letter of 1 Corinthians. We read in 2 Corinthians 8:9, "For you know the grace of our Lord Jesus Christ, that though He was rich, yet for your sake He became poor, so that you through His poverty might become rich."

Paul roots the motivation for material generosity with each other to the spiritual generosity we see in Christ. Jesus had all of heaven as his divine right, the earth as a footstool, all things under him, for him, and because of him, yet he condescended in humility to save the very creatures who would nail him to a cross. In humility he emptied himself to fill us with joy everlasting because of the cross (Phil. 2:3–8). Paul points to undeserved grace and unconditional love as our motive for unreserved generosity. We love because he first loved us. We give because his grace gave us what we didn't deserve. The gospel represents his sacrifice, and in response we offer ourselves as living sacrifice back to him.

It is God's will for us as Christians that we reject the way the world loves, hoards, and views money. We see ourselves as managers of whatever God gives us, motivated by the grace of God through Jesus Christ. The missionary George Müller said, "God judges what we give by what we keep." That is helpful for my own heart, and I hope it is for yours as well.

6. Be a Witness

I remember a time when I was deathly afraid to share the gospel and be direct with people about my faith. It always felt awkward and forced. It didn't matter whether somebody seemed open to talking about religion; I would convince myself that it wasn't necessary to bring it up. If an opportunity conveniently presented itself and I did muster the courage to mention my faith, I would talk about it in shallow ways or try too hard to be clever.

I can't remember when the concept of being a witness clicked for me, but over the years being bold about the gospel started to become more natural. Zeal for sharing the truth feels as normal for me now as eating, sleeping, and breathing. Being a witness became *normal*. That word is key.

I used to think that only people who were "gifted in evangelism" could share the gospel. The rest of us just encouraged them and tried to stay out of the way. But the more I read the Bible, the clearer it seems to me that every Christian is called to be a witness, is gifted with the power of the Holy Spirit to live as a witness, and is absolutely, positively, unequivocally expected to live out the gospel as a bright light in a dark world.

This is what Jesus told his normal, average, undereducated disciples when he left them with the Great Commission. Matthew 28:18–20 says, "And Jesus came up and spoke to them, saying, 'All authority in heaven and on earth has been given to Me. Go, therefore, and make disciples of all the nations, baptizing them in the name of the Father and the Son and the Holy Spirit, teaching them to follow all that I commanded you; and behold, I am with you always, to the end of the age.'"

There it is! Any way you slice it, you come out with the same command. Jesus calls his disciples to make disciples, baptize disciples, and teach disciples. How would we apply this to knowing and walking in God's will? If you aren't sharing the gospel, making disciples, baptizing disciples, and teaching disciples, then you aren't walking in God's will. You can get the best job, move to the most beautiful country, live in the most stylish home, swim in your resort-style pool, and experience all the best material things life can offer while being disobedient to the will of God and not walking in it (even if you think you are) because you are not sharing the gospel.

If you're a Christian, that is why you're here. Romans 10:14–17 speaks to our being plan A as God uses our faithful witness to save souls and change lives. Paul tells the church, "How then will they call on Him in whom they have not believed? How will they believe in Him whom they have not heard? And how will they hear without a preacher? How will they preach unless they are sent? Just as it is written, 'How beautiful are the feet of those who bring good news of good things!' However, they did not all heed the good news; for Isaiah says, 'Lord, who has believed our report?' So faith comes from hearing, and hearing by the word of Christ" (NASB 1995).

The Puritan William Perkins once said that it is the "highest commission to redeem souls from the power of hell and from the grip of the devil."

7. Be Spirit-Filled

Ephesians 5:15–28 is one of several explicit texts in the New Testament where we read directions from God's Word that link directly to the idea of walking in God's will. Once we understand this passage, we know without a shadow of a doubt that it is the will of God for every believer to live the Spirit-filled life.

In this section of Paul's letter, he outlines how believers are to live their lives in light of the gospel. To be filled with the Spirit is to be monopolized by him as your thoughts, desires, words, actions, and even emotions are yielded to him. To be filled with the Spirit is to be controlled by or yielded to him. We know this because Paul has contrasted being drunk with being Spirit-filled (v. 18). One is the picture of being under the influence of a substance that destroys the sober mind, and the other is being under the influence of the Spirit, who renews the mind. The literal translation here based on the present, passive, imperative verb Paul uses is "be being kept filled."

This needs to be an ongoing lifestyle pattern. Passive voice means it's done to you. Imperative mood means it's a command to do it. There is a part of this that you must obey or allow. The filling of the Spirit is a continual Spirit-empowered process in which you are to yield to the Spirit's work in your life. You are to be filled with the Spirit again and again and again.

And when you are filled with the Spirit, what does that look like? For starters, you'll bear the fruit of the Spirit. This is why in Galatians 5:16 Paul tells the church: "Walk by the Spirit, and you will not carry out the desire of the flesh." The Greek word for "walk" that Paul uses here is *peripateo*, which means to be "occupied." This means to be so filled up with the Spirit that there's no room for "the desire of the flesh" in your spiritual house. And out of that kind of life the fruit of the Spirit is manifested, which is love, joy, peace, patience, kindness, goodness, faithfulness, gentleness, and self-control (Gal. 5:22–23).

8. Be Faithful

By *faithful* I mean the idea of enduring and remaining steadfast no matter what you're facing. This is another explicit directive from God that is attached to his will.

To the Christians going through suffering and trials in Philippi, Paul does not say, "How terrible! You must have weak faith to be going through such tough times. Chin up!

Start declaring a better life and you'll have one." Not even close. He helps them see that they are normal for suffering—we all suffer. He also helps them embrace the fact that God is not divorced from their situation and has allowed it according to his will in order to strengthen them, grow them, and use it for his glory. Is that easy to understand? No.

Does that mean God is up in heaven throwing a parade every time his people are in pain? May it never be! Psalm 34:18 would squash any such foolish suggestion when it reminds us that God is "near to the brokenhearted." But all the while Paul encourages their faithfulness to be just like their Lord's when enduring suffering. He writes,

> Only conduct yourselves in a manner worthy of the gospel
> of Christ, so that whether I come and see you or remain
> absent, I will hear of you that you are standing firm in
> one spirit, with one mind striving together for the faith of
> the gospel; in no way alarmed by your opponents—which
> is a sign of destruction for them, but of salvation for you,
> and that too, from God. For to you it has been granted for
> Christ's sake, not only to believe in Him, but also to suffer
> for His sake, experiencing the same conflict which you saw
> in me, and now hear to be in me..
>
> —Phil. 1:27-30 NASB 1995

As challenging as this passage may be, I love how Paul does not lower the bar for the Philippians in the midst of their trials but leaves it right where God does. It's so helpful that

Paul incorporates the phrase "it has been granted," because he's saying that it's a privilege God has bestowed on them to suffer for Christ's name. Seeing it this way changes how we approach faithfulness, endurance, and suffering.

If God has brought us to it, we can trust him to bring us through it. Our job is not to try to figure out how to get out of it or why God is allowing it but to be faithful and trust him. I know it gets used in such a cliché way, but I appreciate the phrase "God will never give you more than you can handle." When we seem to face more than we can handle, God supplies the strength we need to endure. He gets glory when our weakness leads us to dependence on his strength.

We will go through painful trials, ups and downs, suffering, anxiety, and a host of other unforeseen challenges that are out of our control. But in all of this I believe it's possible to be both sensitive and truthful when acknowledging that God's will is for us to remain faithful through every hardship we encounter.

Paul writes, "Indeed, all who want to live in a godly way in Christ Jesus will be persecuted" (2 Tim. 3:12). God's will includes our suffering for faithfully living godly lives. This raises a question: Are you suffering, or have you ever suffered, for living out your faith? Is life ever bumpy, or is it always smooth sailing? One of the ways to know whether you're in God's will is to examine your life and find examples of suffering for the gospel. When you experience this, you don't have to wonder *Why, God?!* Because you are in the will of God.

9. Be Joyful, Prayerful, and Thankful

First Thessalonians 5:16–18 is a passage to commit to memory and use when you lose perspective on God's will. It says, "Rejoice always; pray without ceasing; in everything give thanks; for this is God's will for you in Christ Jesus" (NASB 1995). Don't you love when God's Word is so obvious about God's will? You can be deciding between two jobs, making a huge education decision, or just weighing the options in a simple everyday decision and be in the will of God by remaining joyful, prayerful, and thankful.

Some commentators and theologians argue that these verses are referring to how we should act toward others, while others argue that these verses present how we are to act toward God. I'm not one to flippantly abandon a good theological wrestling match, but on this text both interpretations can win when put in the right order. We are called to be joyful, prayerful, and thankful toward God in all circumstances, which will result in a joyful, prayerful, thankful disposition toward others. I think we can all agree this is easier said than done!

To "rejoice always" means to be in a state of joy no matter what we're facing. This doesn't suggest we can't experience depression, sadness, or grief. The Bible speaks to there being seasons for all kinds of emotions (Eccl. 3:1–8). At the same time, the believer in Jesus is not without hope. We have an anchor for our souls whose name is above every other name. On our best day or our worst day we can still look forward to a better day when Christ will make all things new. He is working all things together for the good of those who love him and are called according to his purposes (Rom. 8:28).

"To 'pray without ceasing,'" writes D. Michael Martin, "one must remain in a consistent pattern of communication with God. The word chosen for 'prayer' (*proseuchomai*) is a general one that implies a worshipful approach to God (Romans 8:26). Paul encouraged his churches to make prayer a part of their personal spiritual discipline (Romans 12:12; Philippians 4:6)."[3]

In his commentary on Thessalonians, Leon Morris writes, "To be 'giving thanks in all circumstances' doesn't mean you are jumping up and down with excitement thanking God for tragedy and trial. We must be careful in that sometimes we hear what the passage is *not* saying when we jump to conclusions. It may not be easy to see the bright side of a particular trial, but if God is over all, then his hand is in that trial; his own cannot but recognize his goodness and make their thanksgiving. Perhaps we should notice that 'in all circumstances' is not quite the same as 'at every time.'"[4]

If this is our attitude, we will walk in God's will even when we are walking through the valley of the shadow of death (Ps. 23:4). God never commands something without telling us how to do it. In this case joy, prayer, and thanksgiving are weapons we use to endure. If you find yourself weak in these three things, remember that God also never gives us a command without providing the strength to obey. Ask the Holy Spirit for help. He will provide it!

10. Be Filled with Scripture

A 2014 study found that 88 percent of Americans own a Bible,[5] and this doesn't take into account the fact that nearly every American adult has a smartphone that can access the Bible. Yet biblical illiteracy is soaring. One Barna study done in 2017 on the top Bible-minded cities in America tells the story. "Bible minded" in the study is defined as having read the Bible in the past seven days and believing in the accuracy of the Bible.

When I first looked at the study, I found my city, Phoenix, at number ninety (not a good thing!).[6] Even Los Angeles scored higher, as we hang with the likes of Las Vegas and San Francisco. Yet churches are everywhere in the Phoenix valley. We have several with five or ten campuses, and one with nearly twenty. If the study is right, it suggests we may be cultural Christians—attending church and holding conservative values, but not necessarily being transformed or living in close relationship with Jesus and the Scriptures.

Is it any wonder that the world is rife with materialism, conflict, political wars, vengeance, hate, and selfishness? You will pour out what you're filled up with. It's a fact of life and a basic principle. What is inside flows outside. As fuel in a gas tank powers a vehicle, or an electric charge powers a Tesla, so it is with the Word of God and the Christian walking in God's will. Fuel is what propels. What you know will dictate how you grow and how you go.

Colossians 3:16–17 illustrates this aspect of God's will and how being filled up with Scripture is what God wants for his children. Under the inspiration and direction of the Holy Spirit, Paul says, "Let the word of Christ richly dwell within you, with all wisdom teaching and admonishing one another with psalms, hymns, and spiritual songs, singing with thankfulness in your hearts to God. Whatever you do in word or deed, do everything in the name of the Lord Jesus, giving thanks through Him to God the Father."

It has long been said by mature Christians and heroes in the faith that a Christian ought to be so full of the Bible that if you cut us open we would bleed Scripture. The reason it's God's will that we be saturated with his Word is because that creates the river through which wisdom flows into and out of our lives. My opinion is not inspired by God, your opinion is not inspired by God, and even the most practical advice and pragmatic ideas may be helpful in some way, but nothing compares to the wisdom of God's Word. I know it's not always easy to be disciplined about your time in God's Word. Maybe you lack hunger, maybe you lack direction, or maybe you lack motivation. You're not alone! What should you do when you struggle as everybody does at times?

First, pray for hunger for God's Word (Jer. 15:16; Ps. 119:103). In the Bible the prophet Jeremiah speaks of eating the words of God, taking them in, digesting them, and they bring joy to the heart. Pray for that hunger!

Second, pray for understanding (Col. 1:9). Paul often prayed for the church to be filled with the knowledge of God and with all spiritual wisdom and understanding. We need the Holy Spirit's help. Ask him to illuminate the truth as the Helper and Teacher.

Third, pray for transformation (John 17:17). Jesus said to the Father, "Sanctify them in the truth; Your word is truth." The Word does the work. Let's study it diligently. That's God's will.

The Ultimate Summation

I know that you have so many practical decisions to make each day. I also understand that for many of the decisions you have to make, there isn't a Bible verse telling you whether to go left or right. But based on what the Bible teaches, I know that if you were to spend the majority of your life living out the ten steps I just laid out for you, you will end up right where God wants you. There's one more truth I want to provide for you as we close this section of the chapter.

I believe a phrase from Psalm 37:4 is the perfect summation of these ten steps: "Delight yourself in the LORD." That one little verse will change the way you think about God's will and maybe even change your life. Here it is in context:

> Trust in the LORD and do good;
> Dwell in the land and cultivate faithfulness.
> Delight yourself in the LORD;

WALKING *in* GOD'S WILL

And He will give you the desires of your heart.
Commit your way to the LORD,
Trust also in Him, and He will do it.

—Ps. 37:3–5 NASB 1995

I used to think that Psalm 37:4 was a promise that would get me what I wanted. After all, the passage says, "Delight yourself in the LORD; and He will give you the desires of your heart." I thought if I just delighted in God, I could get what I wanted out of him and he'd do my will! After a period of time in my life when I started to take the Word of God more seriously, I studied that verse properly and realized it means that if you focus on delighting in the Lord, he will place the desires he wants you to have in your heart. He will give you the right kind of desires so that the things you want are the things that come from him.

There's the secret to knowing and living God's will. Delight yourself in the Lord. When your heart is wrapped up in him, everything else will fall into place.

You might think this is provocative to say but I believe it's true: if these ten steps are a pattern in your life, then wherever you walk, you will be walking in God's will. Make the move or don't. Take that job or keep blooming where you've been planted. Choose the school down south or attend one up north. Buy the car or don't buy the car. Invest in that home or sell it. Rent one apartment or the other. Date him or don't. No matter what, if these ten steps are first, everything that follows will be ordered, aligned, reordered, or realigned by

God along the way. In all of these things, delight yourself in the Lord!

Learning to Live

1. Start with simple steps before overthinking complex decisions. There will be numerous complexities to navigate within any given decision, especially when you're choosing between two great options. Don't overcomplicate it, though. Using these ten steps, map out the areas in your life where you need to mature spiritually and which steps need to become a regular pattern in your life. You'll find that major decisions become easier to wrestle with—even if they're still hard to execute.

2. Delight yourself in the Lord. Make this one of the ways you put truth into action. In your passions, ambitions, finances, plans, recreation, worship, and more, make Christ your everything. All of life all for him.

3. Trust the Lord. You may find yourself asking, "God, are you sure that if I do these things, everything will work out? What if I don't like the outcome?" Your response comes down to what—no, *who*—you will listen to. Will you believe God's voice through his Word or will you believe your own? Are you swayed by the opinions of man, or is the voice of God your anchor? Trust him, lean on him, and rest in his perfect power to get you right where you need to be according to his will. Focus on being faithful, and trust God with the results.

WALKING *in* GOD'S WILL

Questions for Reflection and Discussion

1. Why do we focus more on the big decisions that will help us achieve our material goals while neglecting simple, everyday obedience to God?

2. Of the ten steps that are essential to walking in God's will, which one(s) resonate with you the most and why?

3. What would you say to someone who wants to be filled up with Scripture but who continues attending a church that does not feed them spiritually and who consumes content that does not strengthen them spiritually?

4. What danger is there in skipping the ten steps laid out in this chapter and moving straight to decision-making?

5. In what ways do you need to step up in "being different"? Think of work, relationships, sexual purity, the way you talk, your use of social media, or the things you say you love.

Chapter Three

DOES GOD HAVE MULTIPLE WILLS?

I was around thirteen years old the first time I heard specific theological categories for God's will. I recall attending a Christian camp at which a guest speaker unpacked the kind of person we should date and eventually marry. Of course, all of us were at that age when someone always had a crush on someone else and budding relationships were forged by passing notes during class that read, "Do you like me? Yes, no, or maybe." Sharing a Lunchable with a crush was practically breaking news.

My friends and I at camp listened to the guest speaker who talked about God's perfect will for us and how one day if we married the right person we would be in God's perfect will. He said that some girls or boys were God's acceptable will for us, others were his permissible will for us, but there was one who was his perfect will for us.

You can imagine how much that shaped our thinking in the years that followed. We viewed God's will as this sort of multiple choice in which you could pick a mediocre, above average, or excellent wife or husband. Extrapolate that out into the way I began to view every decision and I would be frantically wondering whether any little mishap meant I had selected wrong and ended up in (gasp!) God's merely acceptable will.

Perhaps you have your own story of learning about God's will and the various categories in terms that people use. Some of it can be helpful, but some of it is downright confusing and instills fear in us. At the core of our effort to categorize God's will is a theological reality we have to wrestle with, and that is that Scripture seems to present a multifaceted view of God's will. But instead of viewing this as a cause for confusion, we can embrace it as an avenue for clarity.

God's will can seem like a moving target, because the thought that we can know God's will seems too far-fetched for our human minds. Over the next few chapters I want to shatter that notion and show you that walking in God's will is not merely possible for a Christian, it's entirely probable!

To get this into your mind and heart, I'll help you do the heavy lifting with some weighty theological concepts, but picture me as your spotter, making things lighter and more manageable. This is the focus of our resource ministry at For the Gospel, where we provide sound doctrine for everyday people.

Nothing frustrates me more than when pastors, authors, and theologians bloviate with big theological words and little simplicity. I remember hearing Charles Swindoll once talk about the importance of "bringing the cookies down from the top shelf" in the church. The man is a retired seminary president and chancellor and has been awarded numerous honors for his academic, preaching, and publishing work. He can go toe-to-toe with the best pastor-theologians of our day, but he still makes it a priority to make theology plain and simple. The goal of this chapter and these sections on the theology of God's will is to do just that.

Here are two helpful categories for understanding God's will.

Category 1: God's Decretive Will

First, what is God's decretive will? Maybe you've heard of it before, maybe not. But theologians also call this God's "secret will," his decreed will, or his sovereign will because it is what God has decreed will happen from eternity past to eternity future. God's decretive will is linked to his omniscience (he is all knowing), his omnipotence (he is all powerful), his eternality (he was not created and has always existed), and his immutability (he does not change). What he has decreed will come to pass. We don't know all of this will or every event tied to it. Scripture speaks plainly about this will. Here are several truths about it.

1. Nobody Can Stop It

God's decretive will involves events ordained and destined. Salvation falls under this category if you believe John 10:16, where Jesus says, "I have other sheep that are not of this fold. I must bring them also" (ESV). His work on the cross would purchase the redeemed, which includes the Gentiles who would also be saved. Nothing could stop the work of the cross and what God had decreed it would accomplish. His decretive will is seen in world events unfolding according to his plans. Daniel 4:35 declares, "All the inhabitants of the earth are accounted as nothing, but He does according to His will in the host of heaven and among the inhabitants of earth; and no one can ward off His hand or say to Him, 'What have You done?'" (NASB 1995).

God's decretive will is also linked to our appointed times of death, as he knows the number of our days. Job 14:5 says, "Since his days are determined, the number of his months is with You; and You have set his limits so that he cannot pass." The Bible teaches us that no one dies before his or her time—as well-intentioned people may say. There may be accidents with us, but there are no accidents with God. He is not in heaven surprised, overwhelmed, or caught off guard by any event, whether good or bad. He has numbered our days and knows the number of hairs on our heads, and even in the midst of tragedies that leave us wondering "Why?" he is near, caring, loving, and working all things according to what he defines as good in the end. We trust his will and ways above our own. He knows what he's doing.

God's decretive will includes what some people call "divine appointments." Events, people, trials, successes, opportunities, open doors, closed doors, changes, and more all fall under this category. God's decretive will is something you should know about but not necessarily get worried about. You can't control these things, so just trust and obey him. Do as he commands, stay close to him, and trust him. He's in control.

2. Nobody Can Resist It

God's decretive will overrules any attempt to stop it by man or the devil himself. Romans 9:19–20 says, "You will say to me then, 'Why does He still find fault? For who has resisted His will?' On the contrary, who are you, you foolish person, who answers back to God? The thing molded will not say to the molder, 'Why did you make me like this,' will it?" Paul's simple point is that no one can resist what God has decreed. Now, you might say, "I disobey God sometimes—am I not resisting his will when I disobey him?" Well, that's why we delineate between God's decretive will and God's revealed will in the Scriptures. Yes, his will is laid out, and, yes, in rebellion we disobey him. But more on that in the next section. Let's keep understanding his decretive will.

3. It Can Be a Secret

Theologians sometimes call God's decretive will his "secret will" because while some things are revealed, many are not. When will Christ return? Why did that leader get elected into power? Why did God allow this, or that? Why did he allow Adam and Eve to sin? What is he going to do in your life next week? How old will you be when you die? And on and on we go with questions that only God knows the answers to, yet he is not detached from controlling or permitting these events. The full extent of God's secret will cannot be fully known.

4. It Doesn't Make God the Author of Sin and Evil

Many people jump to the conclusion that because God is sovereign and decrees things, then he is the origin and author of evil and he decrees sin in a way that makes him sinful. This couldn't be farther from the truth. While God has a decretive will, he is holy and without sin, so even when he allows sin to unfold, he is not the one who does the sinning, nor is he the source of the sin.

This can be one of the most difficult truths for Christians to wrestle through, so I want us to dig deeper on this point.

God cannot be the author of evil, for he cannot be associated with any impurity or imperfection. Evil cannot be associated with him. Therefore, his moral character makes it impossible for him to be the first cause of any evil. The Bible is clear that sin, Satan, and a cursed world are the sources of evil. Because of this, God in Scripture distances himself from evil. And while moral and natural evil do exist under God's sovereign oversight, he abhors evil, opposes it, and will punish it in the end (Isa. 13:11–14).

Beyond that, the Bible clearly teaches that God not only permits but ordains all things that come to pass (Eph. 1:10). He doesn't stop all evil in its tracks all the time. His ordination *involves* evil without being the *cause* of evil. This is a classic, orthodox understanding of biblical truth—even if it's uncomfortable for our human minds.

So how does a Christian reconcile with the fact that God ordains evil but is not responsible for it as its cause? Joni Eareckson Tada's remarks are helpful here: "God permits that which he hates to accomplish that which he loves."[1] You must have a big enough God that he can ordain and allow that which he hates (evil) to accomplish what he loves: our ultimate good.

On one hand, the Bible makes it clear that God is sovereign and can ordain and permit evil. On the other hand,

God holds us accountable for our evil actions. Let's take this tension to Scripture. In the story of Judas and his betrayal of Jesus, we see a clear picture of Judas's culpability.

- Judas was reprehensible and demonic (John 6:70).
- Judas was angry and bitter at our Lord (John 12:4–6).
- Judas was a betrayer (Mark 14:21).
- Judas premeditated Jesus' betrayal (Luke 21:37–22:6).
- Judas was a willing and joyful participant in Jesus' betrayal (Matt. 26:14–16).
- Judas was a hard-hearted deceiver (Mark 14:43–45).
- Judas was full of remorse and committed self-murder from his guilt (Acts 1:16–18).

All four gospels vividly demonstrate that Judas is responsible for his evil. The evidence is overwhelming. From his betrayal to his shame, guilt, and suicide, the New Testament demands that you see Judas as the ultimate villain. Jesus says in John 13:10–11 that Judas is not "clean." Jesus holds Judas responsible for his dirty life and wicked schemes.

If the unthinkable betrayal of Judas isn't challenging enough for our finite minds to grasp, the Bible does nothing to relieve that tension because it also teaches that God ordained everything that happened with Judas. Consider the following:

- Right after the betrayal happens, Jesus blames Judas for his sin.

- Jesus says that Judas was not one of his "chosen" (John 13:18).
- Judas was selected as one of the Twelve, but not one of the redeemed (John 6:70).
- God chose Judas to betray Jesus so that "the Scripture may be fulfilled" (John 13:18).
- The Old Testament predicted the betrayal of the Messiah (Ps. 41:9).
- Jesus is not caught off guard by the betrayal and is aware of the plan (John 13:21).

All of these truths reveal that Judas's betrayal was not a mistake by God. The Trinity didn't burst into panic trying to figure out where the friendly fire was coming from and what they would do next. God knew the end from the beginning. There was no plan B. God didn't have to rewrite the script or edit the plan like we have to edit a book. It was always the plan!

You might be thinking, *Okay, I see the evidence from Scripture, but wait just one minute. I thought Judas was still responsible for his own choices. How could God ordain Judas's betrayal and still hold him accountable? Is that fair?*

I believe you are asking the wrong questions. One must first ask, "What is fair for all sinners?" Romans 6:23 says, "The wages of sin is death." Fairness would mean that all of us—yes, you and me—deserve hell for our sin. Just like Judas, we've all betrayed Christ, and God has every right to condemn us. But for the grace of God we would be rightly sent to eternal judgment in hell. Oh, but grace! Grace that you and I are not Judas. Grace that you and I are redeemed by Christ, not based on anything we have done, but based only on his sacrifice on the cross that paid for our sins. By our faith in him we are saved, washed, cleansed, forgiven, redeemed, sealed, and favored by God!

I have often been asked, "How could God ever send people to hell? That doesn't seem fair." I believe it's wiser to first ask, "How could God ever let sinners into heaven? That doesn't seem fair." The reason many people get hung up on this topic is because we frequently make the mistake of absolving ourselves of sin, and like a prosecuting lawyer, we put God on the stand to be cross-examined and questioned. Instead we ought to see ourselves rightly as sinners who are stained by original sin (Ps. 51:5; Rom. 5:12).

R. C. Sproul was once asked, "Why do bad things happen to good people?" He responded with a reference to Jesus by saying, "That happened only once, and he volunteered." His point is that no one is "good." In Romans 3, Paul levels the playing field of who is "good" because the Jews in those days had the same problem some of us have. We see ourselves more highly than we ought to and look down on others as "less thans," assuming we're good but others are not. But there is only level ground at the foot of the cross. As Romans 3:9–18 says,

> What then? Are we better than they? Not at all; for we have already charged that both Jews and Greeks are all under sin; as it is written:

"There is no righteous person, not even one;
There is no one who understands,
There is no one who seeks out God;
They have all turned aside, together they have
       become corrupt;
There is no one who does good,
There is not even one."
"Their throat is an open grave,
With their tongues they keep deceiving,"
"The venom of asps is under their lips";
"Their mouth is full of cursing and bitterness";
"Their feet are swift to shed blood,
Destruction and misery are in their paths,
And they have not known the way of peace."
"There is no fear of God before their eyes."

Paul goes on to declare the famous words of Romans 3:23, saying, "All have sinned and fall short of the glory of God." There is no denying that we are all, by default, no better than Judas and deserving of eternal judgment. If we were to reject Christ and not place our faith in him for salvation through the free gift of God (Rom. 3:24; 6:23), we would receive the right, just, and due punishment for our sins.

These truths, no matter how submissive we become to them, require us to admit that there is a level of mystery to how this works. Scripture teaches that God can sovereignly decree anything and can ordain and permit evil, yet man is culpable for the evil committed. We will not resolve all of these tensions on earth. In heaven, with glorified minds, we will have perfect clarity, but for now we simply rest in the tension of what we read in Scripture and worship God all the more, because who can fully comprehend his incomprehensible ways (Isa. 55:8–9)?

When we encounter tension like this, God does not want us to wrangle with his words, he wants us to worship. God does not want us to fret, he wants us to surrender to the text in faith. God does not want us to try to solve tensions that require divine wisdom to reconcile. Believing hard truths like this requires the Holy Spirit and a humble heart. God does not need our counsel. He is without counselors (Rom. 11:34). He did not send a survey to get our feedback. He wants our hearts yielded to his revelation of himself. This is what it means to walk by faith.

If you cannot reconcile these two realities in your mind— that God is sovereign and that man can be held responsible— your Bible will not make a lot of sense to you. But when you can believe that all evil comes from man, Satan, and the world's system, and that God, who is perfect and free from evil, can still ordain what he hates to accomplish what he loves, you will be in lockstep with the God of the Bible. And if that rubs your human mind the wrong way, don't fight against that—praise him because you have just come to the place of reckoning where you now see that God is not at all like us.

Isaiah 40:14 unapologetically declares, "With whom did He consult and who gave Him understanding? And who taught Him in the path of justice and taught Him knowledge and informed Him of the way of understanding?" (NASB 1995). I have always fallen back on this passage when my own opinions about the way things should be cloud my judgment. God doesn't need my permission regarding what he permits. I am not his counselor or his consultant. That reality shifts my heart posture.

Psalm 50:10–12 is another passage to keep in your mental file that showcases the sovereign authority of God. He reveals, "For every beast of the forest is Mine, the cattle on a thousand hills. I know every bird of the mountains, and everything that moves in the field is Mine. If I were hungry I would not tell you, for the world is Mine, and all it contains" (NASB 1995).

God asks no one for permission. He rents nothing and borrows nothing, nor does he seek wisdom from anyone.[2]

These realities flow perfectly into the next key truth about God's decretive will.

5. It Is Just and Right

You might wonder how it is right and just that some people go to hell. Regarding God's judgment, the Bible is clear in Psalm 19:9, which says, "The judgements of the LORD are true; they are righteous altogether."

The answer may not be easy to digest, but it doesn't change the truth about God's justice and right to forgive repentant sinners but send the rejectors of Christ to hell. God has decreed that people who believe in Christ by grace through faith will spend eternity in heaven, and those who reject Christ or seek to achieve God's grace by works do not have a grace that saves and will go to hell. We may not like the results and we may wince in agony over souls in hell, but our feelings must never lead us to indict God. If our Father decrees it, then we can say, "This is right."

6. God Controls Opportunities through It

We often want to control our own destiny and make things happen. Now, some of that desire is reasonable, since God gives us gifts, wisdom, and purpose to live out each day. We ought to get after it. As Ecclesiastes 9:10 says, "Whatever your hand finds to do, do it with all your might." But aside from our duties, God's decreed will also controls our opportunities.

It's humbling to look back and see how this truth became a reality in my own life. Several years ago I wanted to plant a church—long before it even seemed possible. Not only was the church I was on staff at not going to plant, but my wife was not on board for a few reasons, one of which was her passion for existing churches to have young pastors who can take the baton from aging pastors. We would have such fun and spirited discussions about the balance between the need to plant new churches and the need to place younger pastors in roles to succeed aging ones. Both were important, and we both had our preferences.

I kept pressing for the opportunity to plant, but God kept all doors for planting closed while opening so many other types of incredible ministry opportunities. Then one day the Lord opened a door for a church-planting opportunity, guided us through the events that followed, surrounded us with supportive people, and now here we are! Both my wife and I share a passion for seeing existing churches strengthened and new churches planted, but in the midst of our preferences, we believed God would control the opportunities and make his will clear.

When it came time to get serious about planting, I asked her, "Will you be able to plant churches joyfully, or will your preference for placement at this time influence your support and participation?" I'll never forget her replying, "Whether the Lord allows you to plant, or places you in a role at an existing church, I'm with you all the way and excited for whatever he has for us to do." I look at her now and see the best teammate I could have ever dreamed of. She's all in, all the time, and has been a gifted pioneer even though she has the heart of a homesteader.

What happened to lead us to becoming church planters, now established in Arizona, and seeing God's hand orchestrate it all? I believe that God controlled every opportunity on purpose for a purpose. On the days when I prayed, "Lord, why are we not seeing doors open to plant?" or on the days she might have prayed, "Lord, please open a door for long-term placement in a church that needs a pastor," God was already at work and controlling the path he had for us. We just needed to keep our eyes on what was in front of us and stay faithful in the now.

Maybe you're in vocational ministry and that story resonates with you, but many people are not. The same truths apply to your experience in business, family planning, education, and major life decisions. God's sovereign and decretive will is going to control your opportunities. You don't need to manipulate, angle, or force doors to open. When it's right, and it's his will, he'll open the doors and you'll know it was he who did it. This gives us all the more reason to pray and praise him along the way for doing what only he can do.

I can think of so many moments when I've observed church members experience open doors in answer to their prayers while others were still waiting on the Lord. What has made the difference? If it were left to our opinions, we might say things like "Well, that person gives a lot of money to the church, so they are obviously being blessed." Or we might surmise, "Well, that person is very obedient, so they always get what they want." Or, more sinister, "Well, that person is an opportunist who knows how to manipulate people and get what they want." All of these ignore the fact that it's God who opens and closes the doors of opportunity. Could some of these statements be true? Sure! But to remove God and his decretive will from the equation is like trying to drive a car without a drivetrain.

We often think of Bible characters as being very different from us because their eras are so detached from ours, but the way God orchestrated their missional opportunities is not unlike the way God orchestrates opportunities in our lives. Acts 16:6 says, "And they [Paul and Timothy] went through the region of Phrygia and Galatia, having been forbidden by the Holy Spirit to speak the word in Asia" (ESV). Did you catch that? They are seeking to go be witnesses, like we've already unpacked in the last chapter, but who decides whether the door will open or close? The Holy Spirit does.

In another passage, Paul is wanting to go see Timothy in Ephesus, but he realizes that God has other plans sometimes and opens and closes doors as he desires. So Paul says in 1 Timothy 3:15, "In case I am delayed, I write so that you will know how one should act in the household of God." Romans 1:8–15 is perhaps one of the best descriptions of how God controls opportunities. Paul writes these words in his opening address to the Romans:

> First, I thank my God through Jesus Christ for you all, because your faith is being proclaimed throughout the whole world. For God, whom I serve in my spirit in the preaching of the gospel of His Son, is my witness as to how unceasingly I make mention of you, always in my prayers making request, if perhaps now at last by the will of God I may succeed in coming to you. For I long to see you so that I may impart some spiritual gift to you, that you may be established; that is, that I may be encouraged together with you while among you, each of us by the other's faith, both yours and mine. I do not want you to be unaware, brethren, that often I have planned to come to you (and have been prevented so far) so that I may obtain some fruit among you also, even as among the rest of the Gentiles.

I am under obligation both to Greeks and to barbarians, both to the wise and to the foolish. So, for my part, I am eager to preach the gospel to you also who are in Rome. (NASB 1995)

A number of key terms in this passage resonate with my own heart to advance the gospel, achieve goals, and move the ball down the field while submitting to the will of God above my own—even if I think my intentions and goals are gospel centered. We can see that Paul wants to preach the gospel, we can see that Paul is making mention of the Roman Christians in his prayers, and we can see that Paul wants to visit them. He's so eager to ensure that the gospel moves forward, but, even still, it is God's gospel, and he is God's servant; therefore, everything unfolds according to God's will. Paul simply shares his heart and makes every effort to be zealous and faithful.

7. It Must Be Respected

James 4:13–16 says, "Come now, you who say, 'Today or tomorrow we will go into such and such a town and spend a year there and trade and make a profit'—yet you do not know what tomorrow will bring. What is your life? For you are a mist that appears for a little time and then vanishes. Instead you ought to say, 'If the Lord wills, we will live and do this or that.' As it is, you boast in your arrogance. All such boasting is evil" (ESV).

Once again we come back to the foundational principle of humility. I have to respect what God has reserved for his own knowledge, his own will, and his own decrees. If he wills, then we will.

Category 2: God's Revealed Will

Theologians also call this God's preceptive will because it centers on his precepts, his commands. And while God's will is a subject that you might wrestle with regarding aspects of salvation, free will, and sovereignty, God's preceptive or revealed will is not a wrestling match, it's a road map! You can know what he has revealed and what his will is on so many major decisions in your life if you'll give yourself to studying what he has commanded in Scripture. But there are barriers between people and God's revealed will that I want to unpack, and then we'll finish with several aspects of God's revealed will.

Barrier 1: Unbelief

God's will won't matter to you if you don't believe in Jesus Christ for salvation from your sin, deliverance from God's wrath, and a desire to live your life for the glory of the God who created you. First Corinthians 2:14–16 says this: "The natural person does not accept the things of the Spirit of God, for they are folly to him, and he is not able to understand them because they are spiritually discerned. The spiritual person judges all things, but is himself to be judged by no one. 'For who has understood the mind of the Lord so as to instruct him?' But we have the mind of Christ" (ESV).

Does God Have Multiple Wills?

The Bible is clear. The barrier of unbelief keeps the natural, carnal, worldly person from caring about God's will. We can say it this way: A new heart is needed for a new perspective. A new heart leads to new affections. A new heart leads to new desires. Unless you believe in Christ by faith, you cannot receive a new heart that desires to walk in God's will.

Barrier 2: Biblical Illiteracy

Let's say you believe, but you still find yourself perplexed by the questions of what you should be doing and how you should be living. The reason for this is biblical illiteracy. Since God's revealed will is what he has given us in Scripture, if you don't know the text, you won't know what to do next. God's Word is the key to knowing God's will. If you want to take the next step, check out the article I wrote at For the Gospel titled "How to Study the Bible."[3] It will help you gain more clarity on how to seek God's will. Don't let ignorance or biblical illiteracy hold you back.

Barrier 3: Rebellion

Rebellious people end up in a bad place, and I don't just mean hell for eternity, I mean in the shambles of a broken life that results from stubbornness and sin. But trusting in the Lord removes the barrier of pride and rebellion. Proverbs 3:5–6 is so helpful here: "Trust in the LORD with all your heart and lean not on your own understanding; in all your ways submit to him, and he will make your paths straight" (NIV).

Trusting in the Lord, in his understanding and in his

ways, will lead to joyful clarity. Submission is not a barrier to living your best life, it's a blessing and the key to it. Your best life on earth means living for the glory of God no matter what you face, and your best life to come means spending eternity with Christ.

With these three barriers clear, let me lay out several aspects of God's revealed will:

1. *Commands.* These are things God has clearly said in Scripture we must do, within the context of our own era in the church age in which we are not under the Mosaic law in the same way Israel was, with prohibitions about fabrics you couldn't wear or the requirements of the sacrificial system, because we're under the new covenant. But as the New Testament makes quite clear, the commandments of God, including ones that span the old and new covenants, such as the Ten Commandments, are things we should obey. One does not say "What should I do?" when it comes to obeying God's commands. Any command in the New Testament to Christians about how we are to live should be studied and obeyed.

2. *Prohibitions.* These are things forbidden by God. One example is found in Ephesians 5:18, which says, "Do not get drunk with wine." Another is in Ephesians 4:29, which says not to let any unwholesome word proceed from your mouth. There are many more, but the idea here is that God prohibits things that will harm you, harm others, damage your witness, lead you astray, or lead

others astray. We should look at these prohibitions not as limiting but as liberating. They are a blessing to us!

3. *Warnings.* We would do well to pay close attention to warning passages and see them as God's will for us to become more discerning and more devoted to truth. Though uncomfortable for some people, warnings play an important role in helping Christians align with loving what God loves and despising what God despises. Apostasy and false teachings, deceitful schemes and the pitfalls of temptation—the New Testament is loaded with warnings and counsel for how to resist the devil (Heb. 10:26–31; James 4:7; 1 and 2 Timothy; Jude). Just as a loving father warns his children about danger out of concern for their well-being, God's warnings come from his deep love and care for us as his children.

4. *Judgments.* God's revealed will is also seen through judgments upon the wicked and unrighteous. He will not hold back his wrath upon those who reject Christ; he will not relinquish the condemnation reserved for those who blaspheme his name or who lead people to hell with their blasphemy. What he plans to do is clear. He will judge the wicked, he will lovingly judge and reward the righteous, and Christ will return and abolish all his enemies. His kingdom will be established, and a New Jerusalem, a new heaven, and a new earth await us in the future. God's judgments are a part of his revealed will, and this should bring peace, freedom, joy, and zeal for faithfulness into our hearts because we can know the plan that God will unfold.

How Do God's Decretive and Preceptive Wills Work in Tandem?

In *Biblical Doctrine*, John MacArthur and Richard Mayhue write that "God's preceptive will is God's will only in a prescriptive sense. His decretive will is the perfection that results in actual occurrences. The preceptive will reveals not what God will do but what he demands of people. God has included sin in his plan, forbidding man to sin yet using sin as a means of bringing the greatest amount of glory to himself (Gen. 50:20; Acts 2:23). In both his decretive will and his preceptive will, God does not take pleasure in sin, nor does he absolutely determine to save all people."[4]

They go on to say that "God's decretive will is executed by means of his preceptive will. God's decretive will and preceptive will must be held in tension. To deny his preceptive will is to commit injustice against God's holiness and to ignore the gravity of sin, but to deny God's decretive will is to deny his omniscience, wisdom, omnipotence, and sovereignty."[5]

Key Theological Truths about God's Will

God is a sovereign Father who does what he pleases. If we are going to get a solid grasp of God's will, we must understand this core truth. God is God, and we are not! This has several implications.

1. God Acts according to What Pleases Him

Psalm 115:3 says, "Our God is in the heavens; He does whatever He pleases." There are people who would say that this paints God as some power-tripping deity. I could not disagree more! What a treasure and what a comfort to know that our Father in heaven is in complete control and he does what he wants. There are no accidents with God; everything he does is intentional, and he will use it as part of his ultimate plan, even when we don't understand what the plan is.

2. God Controls All Things

Proverbs 21:1 says, "The king's heart is like channels of water in the hand of the LORD; He turns it wherever He pleases." God is in total control and is the Sovereign over sovereigns. Now, before you say, "Whoa! So he is the one doing evil deeds, making bad things happen, and authoring destructive horrors in this sinful world?": yes, God certainly can bring judgment upon people, and he has many times, as told in Scripture. But when we say that God is sovereign, we must remember what a sovereign does and what sovereignty means. A sovereign is in control and has the prerogative to start, stop, or allow any action. Therefore, while God may do many things directly, there are other things he may allow and other things he'll stop. Sovereignty means power, freedom, and authority. God can do as he pleases and can control anything, can allow anything, and can use anything and turn it for good according to his purposes (Rom. 8:28).

3. God Shapes and Governs Our Lives

Isaiah 29:15–16 is a warning passage declaring, "Woe to those who deeply hide their plans from the LORD, and whose deeds are done in a dark place, and they say, 'Who sees us?' or 'Who knows us?' You turn things around! Shall the potter be considered as equal with the clay, that what is made would say to its maker, 'He did not make me'; or what is formed say to him who formed it, 'He has no understanding'?"

This passage exposes the truth that nothing we do can be hidden from God or is outside his control.

4. Mercy and Judgment Are under God's Authority

This truth is a great comfort for those who find the world to be a place of injustice and who wonder when or even if God will ever make things right and deal with the wicked. It's also a great comfort for those who have been crushed by the weight of the guilt and shame of sin, wondering whether God could ever be merciful to them in the midst of their wicked ways.

Romans 9:15–18 says, "For He says to Moses, 'I will have mercy on whom I have mercy, and I will have compassion on whom I have compassion.' So then it does not depend on the man who wills or the man who runs, but on God who has mercy. For the Scripture says to Pharaoh, 'For this very purpose I raised you up, to demonstrate My power in you, and that My name might be proclaimed throughout the whole earth.' So then He has mercy on whom He desires, and He hardens whom He desires" (NASB 1995). These are heavy words for the human heart, yet it's comforting to know that God is in control of mercy and judgment. It's good that judgment is not left up to us, because we're sinful, biased, imperfect, and unrighteous outside of Christ's righteousness, and we are prone to misjudgment and mercilessness.

5. God Has No Obligation to Man

If God is the Sovereign over all sovereigns, the shaper of lives, the authority over justice and mercy, and if he is in total control of all things and does whatever he pleases, then there is no obligation on God's part to answer to us, bow to us, appease us, or bend his will to ours. We are not owed anything as sinful humans and created beings. For those of us who are believers, he does love us, call us, know us, forgive us, bless us, and treat us as special. We are his children, a royal priesthood, a chosen people, no longer slaves but sons and daughters. Yes, and amen, *and* still we are the clay, he is the potter. He has no obligation to us. We are his sheep, his beloved; we have been given an inheritance in Christ, yet we are never to be entitled in how we approach him.

Matthew 20 captures one of the most vivid illustrations of God's freedom and authority to do as he pleases according to his will and also teaches us a humbling lesson. In the parable of the vineyard workers, the landowner hires dayworkers and comes to agreeable terms with them on their wages. At the end of the workday, he chooses to give them all the same pay regardless of how many hours they worked. The workers who came first were livid that the landowner gave them all the same pay. Jesus explains in Matthew 20:10–16:

> "When those hired first came, they thought that they would receive more; but each of them also received a denarius. When they received it, they grumbled at the landowner, saying, 'These who were hired last worked only one hour, and you have made them equal to us who have borne the burden of the day's work and the scorching heat.' But he answered and said to one of them, 'Friend, I am doing you no wrong; did you not agree with me for a denarius? Take what is yours and go; but I want to give to this last person the same as to you. Is it not lawful for me to do what I want with what is my own? Or is your eye envious because I am generous?' So the last shall be first, and the first, last."

What a line when the landowner says, "Is it not lawful for me to do what I want with what is my own?" That line right there is what we must remember when it comes to God's will. He reserves the right to do what he wants, because all things belong to him—including us. I don't know about you, but that makes me feel free! Burdens lifted because he carries them, anxieties evaporated because I don't have to worry about making it all happen. Perfect and glorious peace because my God is in control. I simply get to go out there today and serve him, seek to obey him, put my hands to the plow in the field he's placed me in, and love him. He'll take care of everything.

Learning to Live

1. Come to the subject of God's will with a humble heart.
He is God, he does as he pleases, he will have his way, and
we are the clay, not the potter. These truths, which we find
clear in Scripture, breed in us a posture of humility. Is there
any other appropriate response when we're talking about the
power and sovereignty of our God and his will? Like a team
that knows they cannot win and must forfeit the game, we
fold in humility when we come to the subject of God's will.
Who can fully know the mind of the Lord?

**2. Come to the subject of God's will with a submissive
heart.** Many nights before bed either my wife or I will sing
our favorite hymn to our littlest ones. From the time that they
were infants, we've been singing this to them, over them, and
with them. The hymn goes like this:

> When we walk with the Lord in the light of
> His Word
> What a glory He sheds on our way!
> While we do His good will, He abides with us still
> And with all who will trust and obey.
> Trust and obey, for there's no other way
> To be happy in Jesus, but to trust and obey.[6]

When we come to the subject of God's will, submission is
a healthy response to the truths contained in Scripture because
that's what those created in the image of God do. We exist

97

because of God, through God, and for God. Submission showcases our heart of worship before our matchless King. We are his loyal subjects.

3. Come to the subject of God's will with a hopeful heart. He is a good Father, and James 1:17 says that every good and perfect gift comes from above from the Father of lights in whom there is no shifting shadow. He intends good for you, according to his will, and he will accomplish exactly what he promises to in your life as a believer. Be hopeful that you can know his will, and his will is going to turn out for good in the lives of those who love him and are called according to his purposes.

Questions for Reflection and Discussion

1. What role does biblical literacy play in our knowing and walking in God's will?
2. Read Isaiah 55:6–13. Make three or four observations about the mind of God and the will of God in this passage. How are God's ways described?
3. People sometimes get uncomfortable with the idea of God's sovereignty and his total control over all things. Why is this a difficult doctrine to wrestle with?
4. What danger is there in building a theology founded upon that fact that man can do whatever he wants without oversight, ordination, and intervention from a sovereign God?

5. If someone were to ask you to explain two categories for understanding God's will, how would you answer that question? Jot down three or four sentences and memorize your answer.

Chapter Four

YOUR VIEW OF GOD'S WORD SHAPES YOUR VIEW OF GOD'S WILL

Davavid Livingstone was a Christian missionary during the 1800s devoted to exploring and spreading the gospel across Africa. It is said that when he started his trek across Africa, he had seventy-three books in three packs, weighing 180 pounds. After his traveling party had gone three hundred miles, Livingstone was obliged to throw away some of the books because of the fatigue of those carrying his baggage. As he continued on his journey, his library grew smaller and smaller, until he had but one book left—his Bible.

Livingstone knew that there can be many good books, helpful books, and inspiring books for the Christian, but only one is a divinely inspired book. He understood what Spurgeon once said: "Visit many good books but live in the Bible."

Three hundred years before Charles Spurgeon was even born, William Tyndale, a leading figure in the Reformation and considered to be the greatest Bible translator in history, died in 1536, executed for his Protestant views and his devotion to Scripture. He was strangled to death, then tied to a stake and burned for good measure. It was Tyndale who defiantly told the pope: "If God spare my life, ere many years I will cause a boy who drives a plough to know more of the scriptures than you do." Livingstone needed only one book. Spurgeon said to live in one book. Tyndale died for one book.

Here I am having written a book and—to the peril of my own books sales—willing to remind you that you need only one book. May we want more books? Absolutely. Can we benefit from more books? Positively. But if we could pick only one, we know which one stands above them all.

What is it about the Bible that has caused smart, talented, influential, even highly educated men and women throughout history to labor, and even die, to proliferate it and defend it? This one book is the very Word of the only living God. The claim made by the Scriptures themselves is that this book, which is a collection of sixty-six books or letters, is inspired by God himself.

My goal in this chapter is to provide you with five pillars that will support your ability to know, live, and walk in God's will. I want you to conclude in the end, just as David Livingstone did, that you must have one book for this journey through life. I want you to have a strong view of God's Word so that you can walk confidently in God's will. To experience that, you will need to have a high view of the Scriptures so that you read them with more hunger, love, gratitude, and purpose than you ever have before. For in them you have all the answers you will need to demystify God's plan for your life and make decisions with confidence.

These are the essentials for a road trip that leads to God's ultimate destination for your life.

Essential 1: The Revelation of Scripture

When Peter was writing to encourage Christians facing trials, tribulations, confusion, and questions about the future, he put a high emphasis on the revelation of Scripture. Prophetic power is something that encourages people because it both foretells and forthtells truth that guides, strengthens, comforts, corrects, heals, prepares, and fortifies. In the same way that you check your weather app every morning so you are confident in what to wear, or in the same way you plug an address into Google Maps so you can know how the traffic is going to be ahead of time, the prophetic nature of divine revelation through Scripture gives you the essential information you need to know God's will and make decisions with confidence.

For Christians in the early church when Peter wrote these words, tough times were upon them and dark days were ahead. They were under one of the cruelest regimes in human history. The emperor in that era was Nero, and he was a vicious persecutor of Christians for mostly political reasons, using them as the perfect scapegoat for the great fire of Rome in AD 64. Many blamed Nero for the catastrophe, so he needed someone to shift blame toward.

Who better than a generally despised group of religious zealots in the eyes of Rome? History tells of great suffering in those days, and now Peter writes to Christians with a lifeline of encouragement. Interestingly enough, he does not tell them to riot and overthrow Nero, or to fight back with the same vile attacks thrown their way. Instead, he calls them to the exact opposite behavior, insisting that they copy the model of Christ, who did not "revile" in return when he was reviled (1 Peter 2:23 ESV).

Peter goes on to point to the Scriptures as their anchor in the storms of life. Naturally, their anchor would be attacked as the devil used whatever means he could to cast doubt on the security, assurance, and reliability of Scripture.

Questions might have swirled in people's minds as they do in ours today: *Can I really trust God when all of these horrible things are happening to my family and friends? What if the Scriptures aren't true? Is he even going to return? Perhaps we need to take matters into our own hands or find a religion of action instead of this one. If there was a God and he was loving, he wouldn't let so many bad things happen to me. I don't know what to believe, so I'll just believe in myself. Maybe it's better to compromise my faith, do things my way, rather than lose my life.*

That progression can go any number of ways, but the devil cheers it so long as it leads to people doubting the Bible, thinking of the gospel as a myth, and dismissing Christ as the Son of God who will return for his church one day. It is upon this backdrop that Peter writes. Persecution was rampant, false teachers were abundant, and the church was susceptible to doubt. Today people often act the same way, celebrating unbelief and casting God aside. It is as common as ever to doubt the Bible, deconstruct faith, and toss out truth because of bad leaders, corrupt government, lies, conspiracy theories that turn out to be true, or personal hurt. Satan doesn't care how you come to doubt the Scriptures as long as you get there eventually.

What does this have to do with walking in God's will?

Nothing will crush your confidence to walk in God's will like doubting the reliability of God's Word.

Peter, under the inspiration of God, writes to bolster Christian confidence in the prophetic power of Scripture and sheds light on three keys to unlocking that confidence. If you'll take these to heart, you will find peace knowing that God's Word is always a divinely revealed road map for your life.

The Nature of Divine Revelation

In 2 Peter 1:19, Peter's appeal to his readers to look to God's Word begins with the words "We have the prophetic word made more sure." This flows from verse 16, which says, "We did not follow cleverly devised tales when we made known to you the power and coming of our Lord Jesus Christ, but we were eyewitnesses of His majesty." What is Peter saying here? He's saying that he and the other apostles didn't make up all the stories about Jesus, and they can take God at his word.

The truth that Jesus will return one day was particularly under attack. False teachers were corrupting the message, and persecution was causing Christians to be crippled with doubt over the coming of Jesus. Peter explains that they saw Jesus and heard the voice from heaven declare, "This is My beloved Son, with whom I am well pleased" (Matt. 17:5); then 2 Peter 1:19 says they received divine revelation that has produced the prophetic word made more sure and that what they have delivered should be listened to closely—especially in a dark world.

In my own simple paraphrase, what Peter is implying here is "Yes, we were with him. Yes, we saw him. Yes, we heard a voice from heaven and we're certain we're telling the truth. But the prophetic word he has given us to declare to you is even more sure than our personal experiences. Now, it's not just we apostles who can trust that God's revelation is true—we all can. So pay attention. It's a lamp for you in this dark world."

When reflecting on Peter's words about divine revelation and how they relate to our walking in the will of God, I can't help but think of Psalm 119:105, which reminds us, "Your word is a lamp to my feet and a light to my path." This is the nature of God's divine revelation. His lamp guides our life. If you believe that the Bible is inspired by God and is the divine revelation of God, then you are one step closer to walking in the will of God.

Paul also spoke this way about the nature of divine revelation and what he received from the Lord to deliver to us. At the end of Romans 16:25–27, he affirms, "Now to Him who is able to establish you according to my gospel and the preaching of Jesus Christ, according to the revelation of the mystery which has been kept secret for long ages past, but now is manifested, and by the Scriptures of the prophets, according to the commandment of the eternal God, has been made known to all the nations, leading to obedience of faith; to the only wise God, through Jesus Christ, be the glory forever. Amen" (NASB 1995).

In this one passage Paul covers the Old Testament prophets and the new revelation given to the apostles like him. They were receiving special revelation that was new information not previously known. He's talking about God's plan to save Gentiles, which includes us, the message of the gospel, the new covenant, the plan of redemption previously hidden for ages, and how we have everything we need to have faith and obey God. Our Father's progressive revelation and the full plan sits in the Bible on your coffee table.

The nature of divine revelation is what Peter used to encourage Christians, what Paul used to encourage Christians, and what I want to use to encourage you when it comes to walking in God's will. Based on what Scripture says about itself, we don't approach the Bible as merely some book and think of God's revelation through the Scriptures as something we'll just get to when it's convenient. The nature of divine revelation is that God has revealed that which was not known before. Without divine revelation in trials, we have no joy. In confusion, we have no clarity. And in death, we have no hope.

God has mercifully chosen to communicate to his creation in a simple way through words. He didn't have to disclose anything to us, but he did. The doctrine of biblical revelation should cause us to thank God all the more because he has invited us into the inner circle of knowledge and experience. Peter connects all of this to a glorious purpose.

The Purpose of Divine Revelation

After speaking about the prophetic word being "more sure" than personal experience, Peter explains the purpose of divine revelation, saying, "To which you do well to pay attention as to a lamp shining in a dark place, until the day dawns and the morning star arises in your hearts" (2 Peter 1:19). Divine revelation will be a lamp to you. Until when? "Until the day dawns and the morning star arises in your hearts." The "morning star" (*phosphoros*) is likely borrowed from Numbers 24:17, which says, "A star will come out of Jacob; a scepter will rise out of Israel" (NIV). That passage goes on to explain that God will crush his enemies and reinforces truths about his victorious plan. What a game changer when we understand it in the timeline of God's plan and how it connects to the purpose of divine revelation. Here are three applications that affect the way you rely on God's Word for walking in his will:

1. Pay attention to the Word. It's a light in the darkness.
2. The morning star, Christ himself, will come.
3. Our hearts will be fully enlightened. Prophecy fulfilled!

Scripture is not a mere flashlight, it's a floodlight! It illuminates the darkened mind, reinforces that Christ will come, and points to all the prophecies God has already fulfilled. So what? When you are making decisions, don't neglect the greatest, most reliable, most proven resource you have. The Bible is a treasure trove of wisdom for walking in God's will.

Peter's words about revelation are meant to paint a picture of how God's story will culminate and remind his audience that the Scriptures are not merely historical information but prophetic revelation and one day everything God has breathed out and declared will come to pass. That should give us confidence in it. This is why Paul says in Romans 15:4, "Whatever was written in earlier times was written for our instruction, so that through perseverance and the encouragement of the Scriptures we might have hope."

If you've been discouraged, confused, disillusioned, or disinterested in the Word of God, yet you have been complaining about not feeling as though you're able to walk in his will, it's time for a gut check. Do you pay attention to the Scriptures like you pay attention to the news? Do you lean into this Book as though your life depends on it? We faithfully and diligently go to many sources to prepare for each day and for the future; the ultimate purpose of divine revelation is that you would know how God wants you to live right now, and what that will lead to in the future.

With the revelation of Scripture and how God's plan will unfold clear in his readers' minds, Peter finishes his thought by going back to inspiration, providing us with a look at the process by which God delivered his truth to mankind.

The Process of Divine Revelation

In 2 Peter 1:20 Peter concludes his thought by saying, "Know this first of all, that no prophecy of Scripture is a matter of one's own interpretation" (NASB 1995). He paints a contrast to false prophets and false teachers by declaring that the Scriptures do not come from man-made revelations.

"Interpretation" in the original Greek refers to the source of something. He explains further, saying, "No prophecy was ever made by an act of human will, but men moved by the Holy Spirit spoke from God" (v. 21 NASB 1995).

He's impressing on their hearts that the prophecy of Scripture is not the disciples' personal opinions, their own ideas, or even their personal interpretations of what happened. Even though the biblical authors sometimes chose to convey different events from unique angles, all of this is by divine design. The process of the Scriptures being given was nothing short of a miraculous event. "No prophecy was ever made by an act of human will" means that no man initiated this or came up with the idea, but the Holy Spirit spoke and moved men.

Jesus is the one who originally claimed this level of divine reliability when he laid out the process of how the Holy Spirit would help the disciples convey truth. John 16:12–15 records Jesus saying, "I have many more things to say to you, but you cannot bear them now. But when He, the Spirit of truth, comes, He will guide you into all the truth; for He will not speak on His own initiative, but whatever He hears, He will speak; and He will disclose to you what is to come. He will glorify Me, for He will take of Mine and will disclose it to you. All things that the Father has are Mine; therefore I said that He takes of Mine and will disclose it to you" (NASB 1995). In this passage Jesus promises the disciples three things:

1. Future revelation: *I have many more things to say, but you can't handle it all yet.*
2. Perfect guidance: *The Holy Spirit will guide you into all truth.*
3. Perfect unity: *All that the Father has is mine, and the Holy Spirit will disclose it to you.*

John 14:26 includes more promises as the Lord Jesus says, "The Helper, the Holy Spirit, whom the Father will send in my name, he will teach you all things and bring to your remembrance all that I have said to you" (ESV). So can you be sure the Gospels are accurate? Yes! The gospel writers had perfect recall, and Jesus promised their testimony would echo his perfect truth.

This is all summarized with what some theologians call "verbal plenary inspiration," and I believe that it is the only correct position on the inspiration of Scripture. The Scriptures were given through verbal communication, and what was written down were the words of God himself. Plenary means "full" and refers to Scripture being the Word of God in all its parts. No part of the Bible is less authoritative or divine than another. Inspiration—as we now have learned—gives authority to Scripture, and it is revelation from God himself. Jesus is unwavering and unapologetic in John 10:35 when he proclaims, "The Scripture cannot be broken" (NASB 1995).

It is the final, authoritative word of our divine God to us.

Essential 2: The Inerrancy of Scripture

One of Satan's most predictable attacks on your confidence in God's Word and in your ability to make decisions in line with his will is to target the inerrancy of Scripture. A classic Christian view on inerrancy is that the Bible is without error in the original autographs and that God has made no mistakes in delivering his revelation to us. If the Enemy can't get you to stop believing that the Bible is divine revelation or that it was inspired by God, he will shift his strategy to undermining your belief that it's all accurate. *Maybe I can't rely on it completely because it's bound to have some errors. God's Word might be high-level truth about good and evil and heaven and hell, but the rest is up to me. Who really knows whether the specifics about how we're supposed to live are true?* Satan is such a cheap-shot artist, and he endlessly tries to cause us to waver in our confidence. Thankfully, God's truth has something to say in the matter!

In October 1978 the International Council on Biblical Inerrancy sponsored a conference in which several hundred Christians representing forty-one churches and thirty-eight Christian denominations met to study, pray, and deliberate over the inerrancy of Scripture. The delegates formulated the Chicago Statement on Biblical Inerrancy, and more than three hundred evangelicals, including J. I. Packer, Francis Schaeffer, R. C. Sproul, John F. MacArthur, and Josh D. McDowell, signed the document.

Why was the Chicago statement drafted? The nineteen articles, each affirming a position and denying a falsehood regarding inerrancy, drew lines in the sand because liberal Christians and opponents of God were growing increasingly influential and many institutions and seminaries were buying into the idea that Scripture, in the original autographs, contained errors and that it was not be taken as God's perfect word. Some still held to the faith but believed that the Word was not completely faithful.

Of course, this was not the first time that inerrancy had come under attack. Since the Enlightenment (c. 1600–1800) liberals, atheists, and even Christian scholars have run their heads into the wall of Scripture seeking to break it—yet some of them continue to find what Christ said to be true in John 10:35: the Scriptures cannot be broken.

In Psalm 19, David glories in God's revelation of himself through the sky and through the Scriptures. He looks up to gaze upon the heavens and sees that they declare the wonder of God. He looks down to gaze upon the Scriptures and sees they declare the will of God. Verses 7–9 of this glorious psalm contain a bedrock foundation for the inerrancy of Scripture. Six nouns, six adjectives, and six verbs in just three verses present truths that we can hold on to when the winds of doubt blow through our minds and we are tempted to abandon the Scriptures when making decisions. Each of these truths not only provides information but also leads to transformation. Here they are:

1. The perfect law (restoring the soul)
2. The sure testimony (making wise the simple)
3. The right precepts (rejoicing the heart)
4. The pure commandment (enlightening the eyes)
5. The clean fear (enduring forever)
6. The true judgments (are righteous altogether)

Just imagine each of these glorious statements as an immovable anchor for your soul every time you face a big decision, doubt about your future, or the Enemy's lies that seek to erode your trust in God's voice. These are, as I like to affectionately call them, truth bombs. They explode in our hearts, unleashing confidence and destroying every lofty opinion raised up against the knowledge of God (2 Cor. 10:5). Let's dig into each one.

1. The Perfect Law

The law of the LORD is perfect, restoring the soul. (Ps. 19:7)

When you read "the law," it's common for our modern minds to skip over this as some old rituals, but it's actually David's preferred reference to the revealed will of God. If we take the Hebrew construction of this sentence, we get three words: *Torah YHWH Tamim*, which translates to "Law, LORD, perfect." The idea of perfect here means that God's law is flawless and blameless, without defect. Why does the psalmist declare that? Because if it comes from God, it is perfect like God. Psalm 119:160 conveys a similar reality, echoing, "The sum of Your word is truth, and every one of Your righteous ordinances is everlasting" (NASB 1995). Not some, not most, but every single one of God's righteous ordinances is everlasting.

Stop for a second and reflect on how walking in God's will relates to knowing God's Word! If every single one of God's ordinances (authoritative orders) is everlasting, that means that what God says will outlast, outperform, and outweigh every other idea, opinion, or thought ever conceived in the history of the universe. If you haven't clued in to why I believe that the key to walking in God's will is having the right view of his Word, now you most certainly will.

My friend, not a word of God is wasted or wrong. Not a single aleph, bet, or gimel in the Hebrew, not an alpha, beta, or gamma in the Greek is out of place. When God revealed his will through the Scriptures, it was perfect. And what is the ultimate proof of God's perfect law? What it does. "Restoring the soul" means "to turn back and cause to return," so this is telling us that God's Word saves.

This verse refers to salvation for our souls, but might I celebrate the fact that God's Word will also save us from a lot of headaches because of poor decisions? Can we apply the saving aspect of God's precious Word to a host of rescue operations? Yes, he saves our souls through the powerful proclamation of the gospel (Rom. 10:17), but how many times has God's Word also saved us from ourselves? Lies can't save! Error cannot transform! But God's Word does and will. So why does inerrancy matter? Because salvation matters. And salvation matters for our understanding of God's will.

2. The Sure Testimony

The testimony of the LORD is sure, making wise the simple. (Ps. 19:7)

Testimony is the witness of God and his covenant promises. This is what God has testified about, and it is sure, which means "confirmed and supported." His testimony is a house with a strong foundation. The simple person, which refers here to the open-minded, easily enticed, and easily misled person, is made wise. When you build your life on the Word of God and put it into action, suddenly you have better judgment and discernment, you make better decisions, and you aren't taken captive by the next new fad.

In another psalm, which happens to be the longest chapter in the Bible, David is exalting the Word of God and its benefits again and again. He says something we would all do well to remember: "Your commandment makes me wiser than my enemies, for it is ever with me. I have more understanding than all my teachers, for your testimonies are my meditation. I understand more than the aged, for I keep your precepts" (Ps. 119:98–100 ESV).

You may not have everything figured out when it comes to some aspects of life—who does? But read this line twice: give yourself to the Scriptures and your relationship with the Lord above all else. Why? Because it's the testimony of the Lord that makes you wise, and that wisdom can apply to everything in life.

3. The Right Precepts

The precepts of the LORD are right, rejoicing the heart. (Ps. 19:8)

The precepts are YHWH's charges or orders, what he calls you to. I love the way "right" is defined in the Hebrew—it's the word *yashar*, and it means "straight." David is declaring that the antidote for your crooked life and chaotic path is the charge and direction of God. What results? "Rejoicing the heart," which means "to make high the heart and to uplift the heart." Obeying God's precepts makes us happy because we end up living in a straight line. Does this mean your life will be perfect? Nope! Does it mean you will never veer one degree to the right or left? You most assuredly will at times. But it does mean that if you stay close to the Lord's commands, you will continuously be moving in a straight trajectory. Think of a steering wheel making thousands of micro adjustments to stay in the lane of a highway. That is your life when you go back to God's precepts day in and day out.

Nobody knew this better than David. He committed adultery with Bathsheba and used his position as king to abuse his authority and influence. David then killed Bathsheba's husband, Uriah, in an attempt to cover up his sin. That is a powerful lesson about how lying to cover up sin becomes a vicious cycle in which sin begets sin that begets sin. Eventually David was pierced to the heart because of his sin; he lamented about how sin weighed down his soul and drained his strength until he repented and turned to the Lord (Ps. 32:3–4, 10–11). After he did, joy filled his heart again.

This is what the precepts of the Lord do. They correct you, direct you, and convict you, but also, when you repent and turn from your sin, when you give up your way for God's way, when you finally get sick and tired of your crooked path that never seems to lead anywhere, he fills your heart with joy and sets you on the straight and narrow way.

Are you short on joy because of past decisions? Have you been crippled by confusion and you can't seem to shake the fog about your future? Is something just not right within your soul? Do you keep jerking the wheel of your life this way and that? Look to his precepts. They'll set your course and give you joy.

4. The Pure Commandment

The commandment of the LORD is pure, enlightening the eyes. (Ps. 19:8)

Pure is a Hebrew word used to describe threshed grain; threshing is a repeated process of separating wheat from chaff, which eventually leaves you with pure grain. The commandments of the Lord are like grain—or we could even say gold—from which all impostors and impurities have been cleared away. His commandments silence lies and amplify the truth, which results in "enlightening the eyes." This is illumination, whereby God opens our eyes to the truth we desperately need to see. This is one of the key ministries of the Holy Spirit and something every Christian should experience every day.[1]

A correlated truth is found in Psalm 36:9, where we read, "For with You is the fountain of life; in Your light we see light" (NASB 1995). This is what the inerrant Word of God does. A bad map can't lead you to your destination. Wrong directions lead you astray. But God's Word brightens your life and guides your path. It gives you hope and reveals all that God has planned and purposed for you. You don't have to wander in the dark, or wonder what to do, or wallow in self-pity. No matter what challenges you face, what depression looms, what anxieties plague you, what doubts you have, or what questions you need answered, there is no lie in the Book of books, and no errors in God. He will light your path.

Whether it be because of a cold heart, sinful decisions, or your own pride, when you are in the dark, God's Word will enlighten your eyes.

5. The Clean Fear

The fear of the LORD is clean, enduring forever. (Ps. 19:9)

At first glance, "fear" seems out of place in this passage because it's the only noun that doesn't look like the others, but it has to do with the effects of God's Word on the human heart and the way the Scriptures teach the fear of the Lord. Derek Kidner writes, "*Precepts* and *commandment* indicate the precision and authority with which God addresses us, while *fear*, or reverence, emphasizes the human response fostered by his word."[2]

The idea here is that his law is without defilement, and the fear of the Lord through it leads to our being cleansed. Even now in the new covenant, the law exposes our need for Christ because we are unable to keep it perfectly. We do sin, yet we have an advocate in Christ, who kept the whole law, fulfilled the law, and became sin for us that we might become the righteousness of God in him.

In this verse, as in the others, a verb describes the lasting results of God's Word and that it endures forever. God's truth stands. It is inerrant, incomparable, indestructible, and invaluable. A priceless treasure and prophetically perfect. The prophetic accuracy of Scripture is one of the best proofs for its inerrancy.

Peter W. Stoner, a scientist and mathematician, used what he called the "principle of probability" to test the enduring reliability of the Bible. Space doesn't allow me to unpack all of them, but his probability principle was applied to just eight of the more than three hundred prophecies that Christ fulfilled on earth. The math for one man fulfilling just eight historically verified prophecies from hundreds and hundreds of years before his birth the way Christ did was all calculated, and then Stoner multiplied together all these probabilities to produce a number (rounded off) of 1 times 10 to the 28th power. Dividing this number by an estimate of the number of people who have lived since the time of these prophecies (88 billion) produces a probability of all eight prophecies being fulfilled accidentally in the life of one person. That probability is 1 in 10 to the 17th or 1 in 100,000,000,000,000,000,000. That's one in one hundred quadrillion!

I appreciate Stoner's work; it's fun for math nerds and investigators. But in the end all of these numbers prove one simple thing: God's enduring truth will last, every prophecy will come true, and you can bet your life on his Word, because it is absent of any lies.

6. The True Judgments

The judgments of the LORD are true; they are righteous altogether. (Ps. 19:9)

The ESV translates "judgments" as "the rules" of the Lord, meaning his decrees. Psalm 119:160 is helpful here once more when it says, "Every one of Your righteous ordinances is everlasting" (NASB 1995). I can't help but think of Jesus' words in Matthew 5:17–18 when he says, "Do not think that I came to abolish the Law or the Prophets; I did not come to abolish but to fulfill. For truly I say to you, until heaven and earth pass away, not the smallest letter or stroke shall pass from the Law until all is accomplished" (NASB 1995). That means not one iota will pass! Isaiah 40:8 says, "The grass withers, the flower fades, but the word of our God stands forever." And this is where we must all come to choose what we will listen to, whom we will listen to, and what we will allow to influence our decisions. Will you listen to the propaganda, lies, and noise of this dark world, or will you trust the inerrant, everlasting decrees of the only true God?

If his judgments are righteous altogether, it means that he is always right. Which means for some of you reading this that it's time to admit you're wrong. You're a great sinner in need of a greater Savior. Some of your decisions have led to destructive patterns, but guess what? God is the God who can turn your situation around. What should you do? Turn away from your sin, believe in Jesus Christ, submit yourself to God, and your soul will be restored. He will make you wise, enlightening your heart and filling you with joy. For others reading this, it's not destruction that you've experienced but distraction. I want to challenge you. It's time not only to say you believe inerrancy is true but also to live like you believe it is true.

Essential 3: The Sufficiency of Scripture

The final pillar that we must stand upon if we're going to walk in God's will is the sufficiency of Scripture. We're back to where we began, moving now from "all Scripture is inspired by God" to what Paul goes on to say in 2 Timothy 3:16–17: "All Scripture is inspired by God and profitable for teaching, for reproof, for correction, for training in righteousness; so that the man of God may be adequate, equipped for every good work" (NASB 1995).

Nothing summarizes this doctrine as well as the Latin phrase *sola scriptura*, which translates to "Scripture alone" and means that for the Christian, when push comes to shove, when tradition seeks to triumph over truth, perhaps when abusive leaders twist the text to manipulate people unfairly, or when our feelings try to force their way into the driver's seat of our lives, we remind ourselves, "I will live my life, set my course, and trust God's voice to guide my way by Scripture alone. It is enough for me to live out my purpose to glorify God in this life."

Paul says this about Scripture:

1. It is profitable for teaching.
2. It is profitable for reproof.
3. It is profitable for correction.
4. It is profitable for training.

Let's unpack each one of these as we hit the home stretch of this chapter.

1. Profitable for Teaching

Profitable (the Greek word is *ophelimos*) means advantageous and beneficial. *Teaching* (the Greek word is *didaskalia*) here is the content of the teaching, not the act. You could say that all Scripture gives you the advantage of doctrinal understanding. It makes you wise in the ways of God and helps you know the will of God. This is why doctrine matters. Preaching matters. People go to church for many reasons, but the number one reason is that doctrine is taught faithfully because it builds us up. There are many other wonderful things about church that are sweet gifts from God, but if Scripture doesn't flow as from a wellspring of divine wisdom into your soul when you gather with the people of God, it's like having dessert for dinner. Sweet, but you'll soon be malnourished.

In 1 Timothy 4:13–16, Paul exhorts Timothy to prioritize the teaching of sound doctrine, and to recognize what it does for people, telling him, "Until I come, give attention to the public reading of Scripture, to exhortation and teaching. Do not neglect the spiritual gift within you, which was bestowed on you through prophetic utterance with the laying on of hands by the presbytery. Take pains with these things; be absorbed in them, so that your progress will be evident to all. Pay close attention to yourself and to your teaching; persevere in these things, for as you do this you will ensure salvation both for yourself and for those who hear you" (NASB 1995). This passage tells us exactly why doctrine matters and why our pastors should prioritize it in their ministries: because it teaches and exhorts (or gives strong encouragement to) people in their faith. This is why people say, "I have grown so much since sitting under sound doctrinal teaching." The phrase "Take pains with these things" means to be wrapped up in them, diligent in them, and devoted to them. What things? Doctrinal teaching. In verse 16 we see the incredible results for both the preacher and the people: "you will ensure salvation both for yourself and for those who hear you."

How do we apply this to our lives? We embrace sound

doctrine and solid teaching as the key to knowing God's will. It won't always be easy to do what we know. Even Paul struggled with doing the right thing because of sin (Rom. 7:19–25), but knowing is half the battle!

On a personal level, as a pastor this is so convicting for me. I'll be completely honest with you: if I don't preach doctrine and tell you like it is, then stop listening to my sermons, reading my books, listening to my podcast, or watching my videos. Teaching is what we need, and Scripture provides the content of our teaching. If that's what flows into your life consistently, you will be a river of wisdom when it comes to walking in God's will and making decisions.

2. Profitable for Reproof

As you seek to make decisions about your life and to correct your mistakes, you need strong convictions. The Bible is sufficient for that. *Reproof* (the Greek word is *elegmos*) is a rebuke or reprimand. Whether it's by God's Word directly telling you that you're wrong or by someone in your life who lovingly shows you in God's Word that you're wrong, you need reproof. Scripture will straighten you out.

Anyone who works out can tell you that strength comes through resistance. Muscle fibers are broken down to be built back stronger. Pain comes before progress. We see this in the wisdom of Proverbs and in Paul's ministry. Proverbs 27:6 says, "Faithful are the wounds of a friend, but deceitful are the kisses of an enemy." Your true friends tell you the truth and reprove you from Scripture. That's love!

First Timothy 5:20 warns, "As for those who persist in sin, rebuke them in the presence of all, so that the rest may stand in fear" (ESV). This passage is about elders who are needing to be confronted in their sin. Even church leaders need reproof when in continual unrepented sin. Biblical preaching and teaching include reproof. Paul reiterates in 2 Timothy 4:2, "Preach the word; be ready in season and out of season; reprove, rebuke, and exhort, with complete patience and teaching" (ESV).

God's Word is good for us. We need truth to transform our lives and renew our minds. Sometimes our knee-jerk response to reproof is to hate it because we hate to be exposed. But that's where healing, course correction, and hope begin! My challenge to you is this: learn to love reproofs. Even thank God for them. Reproofs are part of the charting and recharting of your course in God's will.

Say this prayer each time you are reproved: "God, thank you for using the chisel of reproof to shape me into your image, get my feet back on your path, and use me for your glory. I receive your loving reproof."

3. Profitable for Correction

The Greek word Paul uses for *correction* is used only this one time in the New Testament, and it means to put something in proper position. Scripture doesn't just tell you, "You're wrong!" It is sufficient to show you how to get right. What a gracious gift that Scripture tells us how to get on track. We can also apply this to how we help others. We don't just call out sin, we point to righteousness. We don't merely criticize someone's faults, we come alongside them and point them to Christ. This is a gift, and it keeps us from wandering away from truth.

I love Psalm 119:9–11, which says, "How can a young man keep his way pure? By keeping it according to Your word. With all my heart I have sought You; do not let me wander from Your commandments. I have treasured Your word in my heart, so that I may not sin against You."

There is a negative side and a positive side. Sin is real, reproof is needed, but God's Word is sufficient for keeping us from wandering too far. His counsel offers us the correction we need. And that correction is part of how we find balance in our biblical counseling of others. When it comes to walking in God's will and telling others how to do it, we must watch the way we counsel.

We can be right in our doctrine but wrong in our delivery. Worse, though, we can be right in theological information but way off in our practical application.

Consider Job 11. (Take a moment to grab your Bible if you're able to. I really want you to see this one for yourself.)

The sufficiency of Scripture is a prominent theme in preaching and biblical counseling, and rightfully so, because the Bible speaks to so many of the issues we face. I don't think we should look to just pop a pill in haste or jump to psychological conclusions about everything. In many cases we should think spiritually much more often than we do, but there is also a danger in dogmatically thinking we know how to diagnose every issue and blanketing things by saying, "Well, you just need Scripture, and you won't be depressed." Or perhaps your special-needs situation is counseled with "Your child just has a heart issue." Or you're suffering and in a season of severe trial, burden, anxiety, and hopelessness, as Job was, and someone comes along with theology and sledgehammers your weary soul. This is the stuff that counseling nightmares are made of, and it derails more people and misrepresents God's will more than we might imagine.

I want to introduce you to Job's friend Zophar. Zophar is theologically astute. Zophar's counseling is biblical, doctrinal, and theologically orthodox, but that's what makes him so dangerous. His counsel in chapter 11 teaches us that just because Scripture is sufficient doesn't mean we hammer people with God's rules when they are wrestling with challenges. Job is suffering, and his friends are offering their advice. Zophar throws in his two cents: "Then Zophar the Naamathite responded, 'Shall a multitude of words go unanswered, and a talkative man be acquitted? Shall your boasts silence people? And will you scoff, and no one rebuke?'" (vv. 1–3). His counsel here is what my friend Austin Duncan referred to as "ready, fire, aim" in a sermon I heard him preach on this text.[3] Zophar goes off without thinking and applies without pondering. He thinks Job should be quiet and that all the turmoil he's encountered is his fault. This is, as Austin called it, "his reckless rebuke." Zophar continues in verses 4–6: "For you have said, 'My teaching is pure, and I am innocent in your eyes.' But if only God would speak, and open His lips against you, and show you the secrets of wisdom!"

Zophar thinks Job has some secret sin and that's why God allowed so many bad things to happen to him. In the verses that follow, he makes more counseling mistakes by going on a tangent about theology. He says true things, but in the wrong situation.

We can learn from Zophar's bad example. We need to ensure that our counsel is biblical and that we're applying it well. We may not always find a specific verse about every specific problem, but we can always find a principle or guideline that can apply to our situation or someone else's. Those principles and guidelines are "profitable for correction" as we live out—and help others live out—God's will.

4. Profitable for Training

Rounding out his point, Paul uses a term that means discipline. As a child is brought up by a parent, or an athlete follows a training plan to achieve a goal, we are brought to maturity of faith by Scripture. When we submit to Scripture as our ultimate authority, the Holy Spirit uses it to change our lives. As we discern God's will for our lives, we can know what is right, discern what is not right, be shown how to get it right, and the results can be that we stay right! Second Timothy 3:17 is where this all leads for Timothy. It's what Paul wants for him, and it's certainly what I want for all of us: "That the man or woman of God may be fully capable, equipped for every good work."

I think of Ephesians 4:11–14 and how saints are equipped by the Word for the work of service and the building up of the body of Christ. Do you know or remember the results of that? Ephesians 4:14 (ESV) says, "So that we may no longer be children, tossed to and fro by the waves and carried about by every wind of doctrine, by human cunning, by craftiness in deceitful schemes."

To believe in the sufficiency of Scripture is to hold the Word of God above every other word. If you do that, it will protect you, mature you, equip you, and God's power will work through you because the Word is enough for you.

As the Protestant Reformation took shape more than five hundred years ago, and people began to realize the historic moment they were witnessing as a result of Martin Luther's Ninety-Five Theses and his challenging of Roman Catholic abuses, he was asked to explain how it all was coming about. He famously responded, "I simply taught, preached, and wrote God's word. Otherwise, I did nothing and then I slept . . . and the word so greatly weakened the papacy that never a prince and never an emperor inflicted such damage upon it. I did nothing. The word did it all."

I pray that one day your life is a beacon of gospel hope and that you would bear the marks of the Lord's blessing and favor in all the ways that money can't buy and this world can never steal. When others ask you, "Why is your life the way it is? How did you end up so blessed and full of peace, joy, hope, and clarity?" you can say without any air of pride or self-exaltation: "The Word did it all."

Learning to Live

1. Load up on wisdom from the well of Scripture. Everybody knows how a well works. A good well is a deep, full, life-giving reservoir from which people can drink time and time again. In light of what Scripture is and where it comes from, we ought to think of it as a well and load up on the living water it provides. When Colossians 3:16 (ESV) says to "let the word of Christ dwell in you richly," it's conveying the idea of being so saturated with the Word of God that you can't help but walk in the will of God. Load up on Scripture! It'll be like building your own well from which you can draw wisdom time and time again.

2. Make decisions according to truths derived from Scripture. Opinions will abound, feelings will soar, then fade, but God's Word will always keep you on a steady course. Love it, read it, study it, and live it! What if we made all our life decisions according to truths that we derived from Scripture? Can you imagine how our lives would be shaped by God's divine decrees and biblical principles?

Think about dating, marrying, parenting, working, calendaring, spending, saving, giving, vacationing, moving, mourning, planning, recreating, devoting, worshiping, prioritizing, disciplining, rejoicing, resting, and more! All of these should all have the fingerprints of Scripture all over them. If it's God's Word, it can guide us toward God's will.

3. Respond humbly to correction by the authority of Scripture. Have you been going about trying to find God's will in all the wrong ways? Have you been trusting in yourself and not the Lord? Have you been following your heart rather than his? Embrace the course corrections that God's Word brings. This application is so helpful because, since we're not perfect, we don't always respond the right way initially when confronted with our sin and called to turn from a wayward path. That's ultimately an authority issue.

If we say we believe the Bible, yet we do not submit to its authority, we're like the man described in James 1:23 who is said to be a "hearer" but not a "doer." We are self-deceived. But when we respond to the authority of Scripture with humility, it will change everything for us—and protect us from our worst enemy: pride. If someone brings Scripture, rightly interpreted and rightly applied, let's make it our goal to simply say: "You're right, because the Word you just brought is right." Scripture teaches that humility like that receives grace and that the unmerited favor and blessing of God will always rest on those who are submissive to Scripture. What a gift!

Questions for Reflection and Discussion

1. Many professing Christians (maybe even you) say they believe in the truths that I have outlined in this chapter, but their actions belie their claim. Why is it so important to examine our lifestyle, decisions, and actions with humility before the Lord?

2. In your own words, describe how your view of God's Word affects your view of God's will.

3. Why does the devil aggressively attack the inerrancy of Scripture?

4. How do we correct those we love while not being harsh or needlessly self-righteous in our delivery of the truth?

5. If Scripture is sufficient for us to live lives pleasing to God and to walk in his will, what place do books, personal experiences, and even helpful opinions have in our lives?

Chapter Five

DECISION-MAKING CRIPPLERS

I have a number of friends who have served in various special forces roles in the military and law enforcement, and one of the most common insights they've shared about their time in training, whether with the Navy SEALs, the Marines, SWAT teams, the FBI, or anti-terrorism teams, is that they all must learn to make decisions under pressure. A close friend on a SWAT team was recently sharing with me about a call he received. A man had barricaded himself on top of a building and was wielding a firearm and threatening law enforcement. The man was trying to instigate officers to open fire because of an unfortunate (but all too common) concept called "suicide by cop" that many people attempt in these unstable times. It's heartbreaking to think of the man's mental health, but far more concerning was his spiritual state.

In the midst of this situation, my friend, who is a strong Christian, worked as the negotiator. His job as a negotiator is to get as close as possible to the individual and begin to talk to him or her. His goal is to engage, distract, and initiate off-topic conversation to get the individual to shift mental gears. He wants this person to get out of the cycle of anger, frustration, or self-harm and into a frame of mind that considers happier or simpler concepts such as food, sports, family, or the weather. Yet in the midst of this seemingly conversational process, my friend has hundreds of topical landmines to be mindful of. If family is a sensitive subject and my friend has not discerned that, things can go bad quickly. In a whirlwind of emotion, that man on the rooftop could begin to open fire on officers, and turn the gun on himself or turn himself in.

All eyes were on the rooftop as my friend engaged in what could be hours and hours of small talk. Pair that with the fact that a dozen (or more) guns were pointed in his direction, a helicopter was buzzing just above, and radio chatter was firing off at lightning speed while he tried to gather his own thoughts and decide his next move. It's a situation that would make the average person's heart beat right out of their chest. Imagine making the most important decisions in life in moments like that. The pressure is on, people are watching; wait too long and it ends badly. Move too quick and it ends badly. Say the wrong thing and it's your fault. Fail to be wise, you end up playing the fool. Lives, reputations, and relationships all hung in the balance based on the decisions that my friend and his team made on that rooftop.

That day, after calming the man down and reasoning with him, my friend did all he could to give the man hope. He chose his words carefully, being widely known in his department for flawless execution in these situations. Some days he's the hero, other days nothing he does can stop someone from taking his or her own life, which was the heartbreaking outcome on that dreadful day.

If you were a civilian living in that building, wouldn't you want my friend to be a good decision-maker? Wouldn't it alleviate at least some of your anxiety to know that he was not a liability when the stakes were so high? I'm sure you would agree that people like him need to be trained to overcome the decision-making cripplers I am going to walk you through in this chapter. And guess what? You need to be as well.

No, you may not be a negotiator for a SWAT team or a Navy SEAL, but your decisions affect lives, reputations, relationships, futures, outcomes, and more. Sound like a lot of pressure? It is, but instead of running from it in fear, you need to learn to face pressure with confidence. Becoming confident begins by training to make better decisions, and training begins by discovering your weaknesses and assessing the threats, then addressing them with God's wisdom, not the wisdom of this world. I call these weaknesses and threats "cripplers" because they neutralize your confidence and render you ineffective. They are some of Satan's key strategies. Being the cheap-shot adversary that he is, he takes no days off from attacking you and trying to undermine your confidence. But God has given you the wisdom, strength, and protection to overcome any of his fiery arrows. The key is being able to identify what they are.

On any given day we will have countless minor and major decisions to make, but each one matters. Even the smallest decision can have a ripple effect, and a major decision can dictate the entire direction of your life. Does that trigger some anxiety in your heart? Then you need to look under the hood and see what kind of decision-making engine you're working with so that these cripplers don't lead to a breakdown.

Let's unpack these five decision-making cripplers and then apply some key truths to our decision-making approach.

Five Decision-Making Cripplers

1. Paralysis by Analysis

This one is near and dear to my heart because it might be the most common issue I encounter in pastoral counseling situations. People desperately want to know what God's will is for their lives, so when they come to a decision, they begin to analyze. Analyzing a situation is certainly wise. Proverbs 4:26–27 would affirm this, saying, "Watch the path of your feet, and all your ways will be established. Do not turn to the right or to the left; turn your foot from evil." It's clear that God wants us to analyze where we walk and how we walk. But there is more than just one set of eyes watching our paths. Proverbs 5:21 says, "For the ways of a man are before the eyes of the LORD, and He watches all his paths" (NASB 1995). Not only do we need to watch our paths and consider righteousness, evil, wisdom, and folly, but also we should consider that God is watching us too! All of this watching and analyzing is enough to make some people freeze with fear, but that's not the goal of God's wisdom. We should analyze the way we live and the decisions we make, but analysis has a dark side when it leads to paralysis by analysis.

Here's an example.

If you live in America, you're likely familiar with a restaurant called the Cheesecake Factory. If you're from another country, just picture a large American-style restaurant that has a wide range of cheesecakes on its dessert menu. But the menu is much more than cheesecakes. The menu is like a small book with page after page of menu options. It's twenty-one pages long, with 250 options, and that doesn't include their new "Skinnylicious" menu. (Someone should fire their marketer for that name.)

My wife and I have laughed thinking of the time we went there as a family with five young kids. You can imagine the drama unfolding with 250 options to choose from, five kids ages eight and under, a baby grabbing everything she could get her hands on, and, of course, allergies, preferences, and everything in between. If you ask me, that kind of high-pressure scenario should be included in military training! After we'd considered the options, we asked the kind waiter to just bring the kids some chicken and rice, my wife ordered something to go, and I ended up eating mostly bread. Talk about paralysis by analysis, it was that and then some.

Like trying to order off the menu at the Cheesecake Factory in the middle of noise, expectations, and other pressures, in life we often see a plethora of options and run ourselves in circles wondering which would offer the best outcome. Before we know it, we have overanalyzed until we're paralyzed. This occurs when we saturate our decision-making processes with too much information (yes, that's possible), and in seeking to find the best road forward, we end up in a cul-de-sac of indecisiveness. Do these sentiments sound familiar?

- *Both of these options seem good. I just can't figure out which is best.*
- *There are so many options, I don't want to mess this up.*

- *Oh, look what so-and-so did. That went well/badly, should I do/not do that?*
- *But what about this other option?* (Repeat question until dizzy.)
- *I wonder what will happen if I decide to do this?*
- *What if something bad happens that I didn't see coming?*
- *I'll just need to research everything and then I'll decide.* (Repeat endlessly.)
- *As I researched, I kept finding more research, and now I am unsure.*
- *I have been overthinking this decision, and now I have anxiety.*
- *After considering every outcome, I find myself more confused.*

If you're trying to figure out whether this is you, just think for a moment: Has your spouse or a close friend ever said to you, "Just make a decision, already! You overthink everything"?

Fear not. My goal and prayer is that this book will bring balance and movement to your paralyzing approach. Every important decision should be analyzed (hasty and impulsive decisions can have horrific consequences), but nobody should be paralyzed!

2. Procrastination

I heard an older, much wiser man once say: "Hard work is usually the easy work you didn't do at the proper time."

Unless you perform hard manual labor as your vocation, isn't it true that we make things much more difficult for ourselves because we procrastinate?

I was recently driving my car late on a Sunday night when a particular light lit up on the dashboard. It was no ordinary light. It was the warning light that represents electrical failure in the car. I continued home and thought to myself, *Those warning lights usually come on a few days or even weeks before something serious needs to be done.* I was treating it as one would treat the windshield washer fluid light. I procrastinated.

Fast-forward to not more than a day later when the car broke down in the middle of the road—during one of the hottest Arizona summers on record (we broke the record for consecutive days over one hundred degrees). One tow truck, one alternator, and a few other mechanical fixes later, and I was one guilty procrastinator! Thankfully it was just a car, but I was reminded that procrastination brings only temporary relief from inevitable pain. God's will is that we live life on purpose and make decisions right away when we know the right thing to do.

I love this little poem I read from Gloria Pitzer that kindly, ironically, yet truthfully calls us all out:

> Procrastination is my sin;
> It brings me naught but sorrow.
> I know that I should stop it;
> In fact, I will . . . tomorrow.[1]

Can we say "Amen"? God's will may involve waiting, wondering, praying, and prudently assessing, but procrastinating is not part of his will for us. This means we ought to change our minds about procrastination if we've been viewing it as neutral and harmless. Proverbs describes the dangers of procrastination in a number of passages. Here's a short list with some brief commentary on each one:

- *Proverbs 14:23:* "In all labor there is profit, but mere talk leads only to poverty." This passage can be summarized with what perhaps a coach, a parent, or a business mentor has told you before: "There are those who talk and those who do." Notice that mere talk is a lot like procrastination in that we say, "I am definitely going to get to that eventually," or "I should do that but I don't really feel like it yet. Tomorrow I'll start!"
- *Proverbs 20:4 (NASB 1995):* "The sluggard does not plow after the autumn, so he begs during the harvest and has nothing." This passage reveals the painfully dark side of procrastination because eventually our delays, laziness, excuses, and avoidance will catch up with us. Not everyone lacks because they procrastinate, but there will be areas in our lives that are deficient or defective because we have delayed until tomorrow what we should have done today.
- *Proverbs 27:1:* "Do not boast about tomorrow, for you do not know what a day may bring." If the last two passages addressed idle chatter and disastrous

delays, this passage makes a beeline for our pride. In a very real way, perhaps in a way we don't always think about, procrastination is rooted in pride because we are carelessly overconfident. Do we really think tomorrow is so predictable that we can delay vital things indefinitely? Are we so self-centered as to consider as less important what others depend on us for? Shouldn't we be humble and service minded, and make decisions with discipline for the benefit of others and the achieving of our purpose? I believe that God would have us live that way.

A former ministry colleague of mine was the administrator at a church and an extremely diligent worker. She would always execute tasks right away. If we met about something on a Tuesday morning, I'd have an update later that afternoon, and the tasks would fall off the to-do list one by one in what seemed like hours and days. I seldom, if ever, had to push her to get things done or check up on the tasks we'd discuss. One day I said, "What drives you to execute the way you do? It's almost surprising to see how fast you get to things and how you never make excuses." I'll never forget what she said: "What ought to be done cannot be done too soon!"

To this day, that phrase rings in my ears whenever I procrastinate. Will I be perfect in this area? No. But God's Word and standard always serve to call me back to that mentality.

3. Perfectionism

In the sidebar is a brief test I have formulated to help you assess whether you are a perfectionist. Of course, the outcome of the test is not an indictment of you; it's meant to get you thinking.

If you scored a +1 for the majority of the statements, it's likely that you already know what I am about to say: you struggle with perfectionism. This means that either many of your decisions are crippled by a reluctance to decide until something is perfect, or you are constantly making impulsive decisions to achieve the elusive goal of perfection. With either mindset, it's not God's purpose for you to be crippled by perfectionism. He is the only one who is perfect; all that matters is whether you are humbly progressing—one step at a time, even if it's only a one-inch step.

Don't let perfect be the enemy of good enough. While excellence is certainly something we should all pursue, perfectionism is something else altogether. The old adage rings true: "A perfectionist is someone whose pursuit of excellence has become the pursuit of self-worth, rather than the pursuit of pleasing God." Perfectionists must learn to accept that a task is complete to the degree that it is done to please the Lord with their best efforts, and also must be careful to avoid extremes. Impulsive striving is not the solution, nor is indecision until perfection comes. It never will! Trust the Lord to cover your gaps with grace.

4. Shame

In the back corner of your mind, perhaps there is a kind of self-talk that hurls shameful accusations like "You're such

PERFECTIONIST TEST

1. _____ I tend to replay conversations in my mind after church, social events, work meetings, or small groups and beat myself up over not saying everything the right way.

2. _____ I am extremely uncomfortable being in church settings without looking my best.

3. _____ If I cannot be the best at something, I tend to see it as not worth my time.

4. _____ I tend to be graceless toward myself and people who make the same mistake more than once.

5. _____ I tend to be slow to apologize, and my spouse/friends accuse me of not saying "I'm sorry" when I am wrong.

6. _____ I tend to think less of myself when I make mistakes, and it greatly affects my self-esteem.

7. _____ I tend to think that if I do not achieve some level of greatness in my lifetime, I have wasted my life.

8. _____ I keep very low expectations of myself and others so that I will not be disappointed when failure occurs.

9. _____ While everyone experiences some nervousness when the unexpected occurs, I tend to be crippled by unexpected situations and run from whatever I cannot control.

10. _____ I tend to get extremely irritable with people who are not high achievers. To me, they are lazy and will hinder my ability to achieve greatness.

SCORE
+1 = This is me.   −1 = This is not me.   0 = I don't know.

a failure—remember the last time you made an important decision? You'll probably blow this one just like you did then." Or perhaps it's more covert and whispers, "You really let everyone down last time. It's better to just do nothing, decide nothing, and say nothing rather than risk making a mistake." Whether it's with shame to keep you feeling like a failure in all that you do, or shame to keep you from doing anything at all, Satan loves to pin you down with the past. But is that how the grace of God operates in our lives? Is God a shame-monger? Does he enjoy racking your brain day after day with all the mistakes and poor decisions you've made? Sure, you can learn from your mistakes, but God doesn't want you lingering over them.

5. Fear

Everyone has a fight-or-flight response to situations in life, but sometimes we freeze. I remember the first time I played paintball and felt an adrenaline rush like never before—the thrill of being under attack, knowing the other team was coming for us, and the looming fear of what would happen if they rushed us. Having never been in that type of situation before, and admittedly not wanting to be shot with a paintball at close range, I froze, tucked into a barrier, and was eventually shot because I didn't move. Fear of what *could* happen immobilized me. Isn't that what fear does? It's a crippler!

Fear also has another side to it, which causes us to react emotionally and hastily. Sure, we all have those "paintball" moments like I did, but how many times have you been struck with fear of what could be or of the unknown and instead of slowing down to think and be rational, your fear caused you to make a hasty decision or fire off with a hasty reaction? Fear tends to drive quick reactions and emotional collapse, and it is rooted in a lack of trust in God.

One of the best illustrations of decision-making being crippled by fear is found in the parable of the talents in Matthew 25:14–30. The parable is about a man who went on a journey and left his servants in charge of various levels of stewardship, called talents. A talent was a form of currency in those days. He gave one servant five talents, another servant two talents, and a third servant one talent. The first servant went out immediately and, through wise decision-making, turned his five talents into ten. The second servant went out and turned his two talents into four. But the third servant took a different approach, which was largely based in fear. Matthew 25:18 records, "But he who received the one talent went away, and dug a hole in the ground and hid his master's money" (NASB 1995).

As the story unfolds, the master comes home and wants an account of how the servants managed what he had given them while he was away. The "return of the master" represents the return of Christ. When confronted by their master, the first two servants find great favor with him because they were diligent with what they had been given. But the third servant had operated out of fear. He explains why he buried the talent: "'Master, I knew you to be a hard man, reaping where you did not sow, and gathering where you did not scatter seed. And I was afraid, so I went away and hid your talent in the ground.' . . . But his master answered and said to him, 'You worthless, lazy slave!'" (Matt. 25:24–26).

Did you catch the reasoning for the servant's decision? He said, "I was afraid." Do you see what fear does? In the midst of great opportunity, the third servant made a decision out of fear, and it crippled his stewardship. We often think of fear as something that keeps us stationary, as though its only effect is to freeze us in place. No! Fear can also lead us to make foolish and faithless decisions because we're playing it safe and not trusting in God, when God has called us to follow him courageously and trust him consistently.

Confronting Your Cripplers

CSS *Hunley* was a submarine used in the 1800s. (Yes, you read that correctly!) It was named after its inventor, Horace Lawson Hunley (ironically, he died in the test dives). The submarine became famous not only for being the first submarine in history to attack a warship but for its self-destruction after bringing down the enemy ship. On February 17, 1864, the *Hunley* was under the cover of darkness when it attacked a sixteen-gun warship, USS *Housatonic*, off the coast of Charleston, South Carolina.

After the attack the *Hunley* was never seen again. What happened on that fateful night was not discovered until more than 130 years later when, in the year 2000, the *Hunley* was rescued from the depths of the sea by archaeologists. After Duke University conducted a study on the *Hunley*, it was determined that the submarine, with all of its ingenuity and promise, had self-destructed from its own torpedo detonation that night. The *Hunley* sank not only the *Housatonic* but also itself!

The *Hunley* represents a vivid picture of the kind of self-destruction we can inflict when facing decisions. With the best of intentions we muster up the gusto to take on a goal, only to sink in the process. Whether it's through paralysis by analysis, procrastination, perfectionism, shame, or fear, we can be our own worst enemies in the process of making decisions. But God has provided us with ways to confront these decision-making cripplers so they do not derail us or define us. Three particular steps can be taken to put cripplers in their place.

First, confess. We seldom address what we don't first admit. Confession is the acknowledgment that you have a sin issue with decision-making and that your feelings are driving your decisions, rather than what you know. Confess any specific crippler holding you back from making confident, well-informed, God-honoring decisions.

Second, connect. Connecting begins with God, and it happens through prayer and time spent in his Word. Prayer is our power source when addressing weaknesses and patterns of sin, and the Bible is our compass, pointing us toward the right direction. I want to lovingly urge you to consider what connecting with God through prayer truly means: Prayer is not a rehearsal of how bad and broken you are again and again; it involves confession of sin, but it also moves you to seek strength, wisdom, direction, and peace from the Lord. Most of all, it will include walking in his grace. Ask him for help, don't just tell him you're helpless. And remember, use the Bible as your foundation for connecting with God. It will keep your feet firmly rooted in the truth. More on that in a later chapter.

Third, correct. What good is information if it doesn't lead to transformation? Confess your cripplers as sin, connect with God through prayer and Scripture, then take action to correct your behavior by getting to the heart of the issue. One of the aspects of correction that I enjoy, even though it can be daunting, is getting a trusted friend involved so you can be accountable and be encouraged. Nobody can see their own blind spots—hence the term! I have a few friends I share just about everything with.

My wife knows me as nobody else does, and I do talk with her about areas I need to grow in, but I have a few trusted brothers who are strong, godly, and appropriately invasive when it comes to areas of weakness and growth in my life. If I am needing to correct something in my life, not only do I make a plan to grow but I get a trusted brother involved in that plan. My encouragement and challenge to you is not to be an island when it comes to decision-making. Seek counsel and correction. If you have patterns that revolve around the cripplers we've talked about, God has given you the gift of his church to strengthen you in ways you may have never imagined.

As we go forward, there will be plenty of information in this book to give you tools for knowing and living God's will, but let's refuse to neglect the transformation that occurs when we seek to know and live God's will in community with others.

Learning to Live

1. View decision-making as part of spiritual discipline. This turns procrastination into a heart issue so that you can begin to see it as laziness, fear, or carelessness in disguise. When you start calling it sin, you've taken the most important step toward not excusing it. The truth is that decision-making is a spiritual discipline because it's something you do regardless of feelings. You make decisions because they are right, because they are necessary, and because to not make decisions has far-reaching consequences that can cripple your spiritual well-being. Refuse to buy the lie "Tomorrow, tomorrow, there will always be tomorrow." Today is a great day to call out procrastination for what it is.

2. Learn from your failures and then let them go. Failure can be our friend because it teaches us valuable lessons, but it can be our foe when it lingers. Whether it be failures from ignorance, willful acts, or patterns that need to change, many moments of great progress flow out of lessons learned from pain. We have a phrase we use with our team: "Feel pain once." The simple meaning of this phrase is that we can choose to repeat our mistakes or we can learn from them. These three words can be life-changing.

On one hand, you are going to feel pain. On the other hand, you can learn valuable lessons from it. On one hand, there are things you can't control. On the other hand, there are things you can. On one hand, you are going to make some mistakes. On the other hand, you can prevent those mistakes from happening again by planning for how you'll handle similar situations in the future. What if we view our failures more as lessons than as cripplers and definers of our future?

Learn from your mistakes but let them go. Your future does not need to be defined by your failures; rather, it can be shaped by how you respond to those failures.

3. Look to Christ. What these five decision-making cripplers have in common is that they all shift your eyes off Jesus and onto something drastically inferior. Overanalyze and you'll soon find you've let the white noise of this world cloud your clarity. Procrastinate and you've become like the man who says, "I'll do what God wants tomorrow, but today belongs to me!" Obsess over perfectionism and you'll delay obedience to God. Wallowing in shame is believing that God can't ever fix your situation. To cower or hastily react in fear is to declare that God can't handle the situation. These are lies that will lure you away from the Rock of Ages, who is your sure and steady anchor.

Questions for Reflection and Discussion

1. What decision-making cripplers are most prevalent in your life?
2. Why is it dangerous to let fear drive your decisions?
3. Name at least one friend whom you can trust to call you out and tell you like it is in love, and note a time or situation when this friend helped you see a major blind spot.
4. Read Psalm 103:12. Once sin is confessed, how should God's grace affect how we bounce back from guilt?
5. What decisions are you facing right now that can be better made in light of this chapter?

Chapter Six

FUNDAMENTALS FOR EVERY FORK IN THE ROAD

The year was 2014 and I wanted to leave the church I was attending to go to seminary. When my wife and I began having the conversation about the potential move, our first baby was on the way. At that time I was still in the first couple of years of my conversion, so we chose to stay at our church, keep serving and learning, have a baby, and attend a local seminary (though it wasn't my first choice). Fast-forward to 2016 and we were right back in the same conversation, because I'm one of those stubborn types!

My wife and I sat down one night to talk, and I said, "I applied to seminary again and received an offer for a full scholarship. We just need to do it. I'm going in the hole from student loans and at this rate will end up with forty thousand dollars in debt. Life is hard anyway—why make it harder by having debt for seminary? Let's leave where we are, move to LA, go full-time in seminary, I'll work two jobs, grind for three years, then see what the Lord has for us." I was already working a full-time job for a church and an additional twenty-four hours a week as a server. I was also attending seminary and paying for it, so life was a grind already—why not move to seminary and make it all worth it with free education?

Maybe you think we should have made the move, but we ended up deciding that it wasn't right for us at that time. We had two babies, I was on staff at a church gaining valuable experience in ministry, and even though a scholarship would have minimized future debt, we made our decision based on a number of factors using seven *P*s.

Using the seven *P*s in this chapter, I want to provide you with what I would describe as the fundamentals for navigating every fork in the road. When you come to a situation where you are deciding between two or more options, you need to have a plan in place for making decisions. Think about the character of our God for a moment. When he chose to redeem us, did he wing it or plan ahead? When he sent his Son to die, did he know what he was seeking to accomplish?

When Christ rose and ascended, did God have a plan to send anyone else as a Helper? Absolutely! God plans, and we, as his image bearers, ought to as well. Although imperfectly, we can put into practice basic principles of wisdom and prudence to make decisions. This framework for decision-making helped us sift through the fears, desires, ambitions, arguments, and realities of our situation. My hope is not that you'll take our template and force it on your own situation, but instead I want you to see that decision-making as a Christian involves a Spirit-filled, Spirit-led, Spirit-controlled approach. You need to think about the most important things, not just the things you want to think are important.

Without further delay, here are the seven *P*s.

The Seven *P*s of Decision-Making

1. What Is Our Process?

To make great decisions, everyone needs a process. But this will test another (unrelated) *P* we're all familiar with called Patience. Patience is not exactly a natural trait when it comes to making decisions, which can lead to impulsively bad decisions. There are times when we jump into making decisions without pausing to think about our process. Now, if you're one of those impulsive types who just want what they want when they want it, I'm going to bother you by insisting you develop a process, but I have to tell you—I'm just like you! Nothing tests my patience more than having to slow down and think about process when I feel a sense of urgency to make a decision. Yet when we consider that one of the fruits of the Holy Spirit is patience (Gal. 5:22–23), we must ask a serious question: Are decisions that are rushed, impulsive, chaotic, and forced Spirit-filled decisions? I believe the Holy Spirit is grieved when we ignore processes and rush right into decision-making. Now, I'm not referring to delaying obedience. There will be many cases in our daily lives when we already know what decision to make because Scripture is clear. It would be the opposite of Spirit-filled decision-making to delay obedience to God. What I am referring to is keeping our emotions in check and thinking logically, biblically, and rationally about the decision-making process we commit to. Here are some key questions to ask at this first and crucial step:

- Have we mapped out what this decision-making process will look like?
- Are we on a timeline?
- Have we prayed about the decision, and how long will we pray before taking any next steps?

- Who are the counselors we believe could objectively and biblically speak into our situation?
- Have we written out our priorities?
- Once we have decided to pursue a next step, whom will we tell?
- If the door closes, will we continue to pursue this decision in the short term, or plan to revisit it in the future?

These are just several of the questions you can ask yourself as you map out the process, but be sure to add more based on your own unique situation. As with any important goal, breaking down how you will approach it will help you think through it logically. Consider this no different from what an architect does when he or she begins to lay out a blueprint. No construction material has been purchased, no major building has begun, and some of the details are still to be determined, but the blueprint serves as a guide when things start to move, designers get consulted, contractors get hired, and permits get approved.

2. Have We Prayed?

Time and time again, bad decisions are accompanied by prayerlessness. Perhaps the greatest downfall of our decision-making process is not the error of a final decision, since God can turn any situation around for his glory and our good (Rom. 8:28), but our lack of prayer about decisions before making them. Whether it's because we're in a rush to decide or it's simply out of forgetfulness, often because we're overwhelmed by anxiety, we do not pray.

By contrast, a good decision is accompanied by prayer. That investment will always pay dividends. An investment in prayer is never wasted or lost; prayer doesn't slow down progress. Prayer is essential to making great decisions and fundamental to making decisions that God will bless. Those who seek God in prayer will never be disappointed. If you have people in your life who would scoff at your need to slow down and pray about a decision, those are people who should have no seat at the table of counsel regarding your decision. As practical advice on what to pray, consider the following:

- Pray for the Lord's will to be done (Luke 22:42).
- Pray for the Lord to open doors he wants to open.
- Pray for the Lord to close doors he wants to close. (Yes! Pray for things *not* to go your way if that is the Lord's will.)
- Pray for the Lord to bring counsel into your life from those who are wise.
- Pray for the Holy Spirit to bring strong conviction upon you if you are in disobedience.
- Pray for joy in the midst of the process.
- Pray for peace no matter the outcome.
- Pray for God to be glorified in your attitude, your approach, and all outcomes.
- Pray for resilience if you are being obedient to God and experience opposition from others.

- Pray for wisdom if complexities occur.
- Pray for a sober mind if people try to manipulate or control you when you know you are obeying God.
- Pray for the Lord's blessing on your life in whatever ways bring him the most glory (1 Cor. 10:31).

There are two particular prayer passages that I regularly go to when making decisions or facing mountains that only the Lord can help me climb. Philippians 4:6–7 and James 1:5 both provide excellent insight into prayer and decision-making. Let's break them down together under two primary truths.

- *Truth 1: Prayer brings peace.* "Be anxious for nothing, but in everything by prayer and supplication with thanksgiving let your requests be made known to God. And the peace of God, which surpasses all comprehension, will guard your hearts and your minds in Christ Jesus" (Phil. 4:6–7 NASB 1995).
- *Truth 2: Prayer brings wisdom.* "But if any of you lacks wisdom, let him ask of God, who gives to all generously and without reproach, and it will be given to him" (James 1:5).

3. Have We Sought Counsel with Prudence?

People who consistently make wise decisions are typically those who have learned to love collaboration and consultation with biblically minded individuals. No one is truly self-made, and no one succeeds in their plans without insight from somewhere or someone else. I have a good friend who is a wise investor. He knows how to manage money and real estate and plan financially, yet he's barely thirty years old. One day I asked him, "How did you learn about all of this and make such incredible decisions at such a young age?"

He replied, "At seventeen years old I walked up to a college professor who was a brilliant economist and said, 'Will you teach me the most important things about money that a person would need to know?' That day, he taught me about the power of compound interest, and the rest is history." My friend may decide to invest in something or acquire another piece of real estate on his own now, but his prudent mentality continues to pay dividends in his decisions today.

Proverbs 11:14 reminds us, "Where there is no guidance the people fall, but in an abundance of counselors there is victory." If you want to win when it comes to making wise decisions, seek wise counsel. I should note that "winning" at decisions doesn't necessarily mean succeeding. It means gaining wisdom, greater perspective, or peace knowing that you have followed God's Word when making decisions with intentionality.

In contrast to the wise person who seeks counsel is the fool who does whatever he or she wants. Proverbs 18:1–2 warns against the kind of rogue individualism that only fools delight in: "One who separates himself seeks his own desire; he quarrels against all sound wisdom. A fool does not delight in understanding, but in revealing his own mind."

When we think about slowing down to seek wise counsel,

we're acting with what Proverbs refers to as prudence. This is how *Merriam-Webster* defines prudence:

1. the ability to govern and discipline oneself by the use of reason
2. sagacity or shrewdness in the management of affairs
3. skill and good judgment in the use of resources
4. caution or circumspection as to danger or risk[1]

When you mention "prudence," there are some who will think of it as a stuffy, boring, limiting approach to life. They couldn't be more wrong and most definitely could be missing out on one of God's greatest gifts for making decisions in line with his will.

According to the Bible, prudence involves a type of discretion, and it could certainly lead to a biblical view of money, modesty, planning, decision-making, relationships, emotions, wisdom, and more. In the book of Proverbs prudence is mentioned on numerous occasions. Sometimes Bible translations will use the word "understanding," which actually gives us a clue as to the broader meaning of this decision-making trait. If I were to give you a working definition, I would say: "Prudence is the ability to discern and understand circumstances, decisions, people, thoughts, and emotions so that everything you do and say pleases the Lord and bears the most fruit in your life for him."

I want to give you nine principles of prudence from Proverbs that you can use as a kind of devotional study for decision-making. You could even call these "nine blessings of being prudent." What I love about Proverbs is that it shows everyone how clear and achievable prudence really is. New Christians and mature Christians alike can put these principles into practice and experience the benefits of God's direction through his Word.

1. We will not be naive when we act with prudence (1:4).
2. When we are prudent, we are being wise (8:12–14).
3. Prudence slows us down and controls our emotions (12:16).
4. Prudence helps us embrace discipline and be teachable (15:5).
5. Prudence (related to the word "understanding") is the fountain of life, which is the opposite of a fool's demise (16:22).
6. Prudence will help us keep our mouths under control (17:28).
7. Prudence will help us acquire knowledge and put it into action (18:15).
8. A prudent wife is a gift directly from the Lord (19:14).
9. Prudence will protect us from evil (27:12).

My prayer and hope is that these passages become for you what a well-lit runway is for an aircraft looking for a safe place to land. Prudence enables you to think deeply about your decisions and to ask the right questions. Prudence enables you to move to the next *P* in the most advantageous way—fully confident in who you are, why you are, what you hope to accomplish, and what you're living for.

4. What Are Our Top Priorities?

Eric Liddell was an Olympian who become a Christian hero because he was living for something greater than gold. As the son of Scottish missionaries, he was born on the mission field in China. After returning to Scotland as a young boy, he became widely recognized as a very gifted athlete, excelling in both rugby and track. Along with growing into a strong athlete, Eric grew up to be a strong Christian who placed his faith above all other priorities. Life was good, and Eric was fast!

In 1923 he set a British record for the 100-meter dash, which stood for more than two decades, and in 1924 he was heading to the Olympic Games in Paris. In the months leading up to the Olympics, his priorities would be put to the test in a way that few people could have imagined. When the race dates and times were posted, the highly touted sprinter was scheduled for the 100-meter on a Sunday. Liddell refused to run on Sunday because he held a strong conviction that it was the Lord's Day. His priorities dictated his decision.

As a result he was entered instead into the 400-meter race, a distance he had not trained for. His times in the 400-meter were mediocre and disappointing compared with what he could do in the 100-meter. Nonetheless, the 400-meter event was his race, because he had made the decision to withdraw from the 100-meter. On July 11, 1924, Liddell ran the race of his life, setting both an Olympic and world record with his time and securing gold. His testimony went on to inspire countless generations, and he is one of the characters depicted in the Oscar-winning film *Chariots of Fire*.

After the Olympics, Eric Liddell ran his most important race when he turned his attention to missionary work in China. Like Paul the apostle, he would run his race and finish his course on the mission field, eventually dying in service and becoming a hero of the faith. Today, while his legacy has been cemented in the Scottish Sports Hall of Fame and as a beloved Olympic athlete, his greatest legacy stands as a Christian who prioritized what mattered most throughout his life. He lived, and died, for the sake of Christ.

You may not have the same convictions as Liddell, but the same commitment to priorities will benefit your decision-making confidence. Not all will agree with every decision you make, but there will be no need to second-guess what you've been intentional about. Priorities are a powerful decision-making tool. They allow you to think about what matters most to you and make decisions in light of that. For Christians, priorities are ultimately shaped by a love for Christ and a willingness to live for him above all else. When facing a fork in the road, consider the following four priorities.

1. Spiritual

This one isn't crazy or radical. You know it. I know it. The first and most important priority in every decision is the spiritual implications of that decision. Will it positively or negatively affect your relationship with God? Are you going to be in a position that makes it more or less difficult to grow spiritually? This priority can be applied to every decision based on your unique context.

For example, if the decision involves a job transition that would require you to move, you might ask, "Have I already selected a healthy local church in the new area where I will live?" Or you might ask, "In what ways am I currently growing spiritually, and will that continue where I am going or even improve?" If the decision is about a relationship, you might ask, "How will dating/marrying/fellowshiping with this person influence me spiritually? Is the Lord being honored through this relationship or does it expose a weakness or temptation that pulls me into sin?"

You get the point. Spiritual priorities matter. I don't ever make a decision that excludes this consideration. In my flesh I might say, "Oh, please! I can be close to God and make new friends anywhere. It's not about a brick-and-mortar church building." That kind of attitude may be an appealing coping mechanism when facing difficult decisions, but it doesn't address any number of blind spots that still remain if we do not think deeply and carefully about spiritual connectedness.

2. Financial

Stewardship is a key Christian principle and a major theme in Jesus' ministry and in Proverbs. Provision and preparedness are important. You make healthy decisions when including financial health in your priorities and thinking through what matters most to you. This can be tricky because the heart is deceitful and plays tricks on us (Jer. 17:9), but through prayer and the other steps in the process, you can insulate yourself from the dangerous lure of greed while making wise decisions that take into consideration financial implications. Here are some questions you might ask yourself:

- How important is financial stability to me?
- What financial sacrifices am I willing to make for this decision?
- In what ways can this decision lead to better financial stability?
- What will it cost to execute this decision?
- Will this decision help me better provide for my loved ones?
- Am I putting myself or loved ones at risk by making this decision?
- What is my tolerance for risk and why am I considering this decision?

I recommend thinking cautiously and prudently (as we've discussed!) about financial priorities for a few reasons.

First, don't get too caught up in chasing money. Paul cautions about the love of money in 1 Timothy 6:10 when he writes, "The love of money is a root of all sorts of evil, and some by longing for it have wandered away from the faith and pierced themselves with many griefs." What a sobering word from the apostle who knew how to be content with much and with only a little (Phil. 4:11–13). Financial priorities matter, but only insofar as they work within the boundaries set by Scripture.

Second, be mindful that if every missionary, pastor, and Christian made decisions based on the financial potential, we'd have no Hudson Taylor to China, Adoniram Judson to Burma, Amy Carmichael to India, John G. Paton to the cannibals on the New Hebrides Islands in the South Pacific, Lottie Moon to China, David Livingstone to Africa, or Mary Slessor to Nigeria. I am sure glad that they never got too caught up in asking, "Will this decision lead to better financial stability?" Otherwise they never would have gone!

Here we are reminded of the all-important aspect of prudence again, and we see how each of these *Ps* work within the larger framework. We are never to swing to extremes or forget that each major decision requires logic. In some cases you will have a strong conviction to go to the mission field and the financial questions will revolve around whether God has begun providing for your specific work. Or you may be focused on obtaining a good job, providing for your family, and giving to missionaries through your God-given first-world income, so you'll consider how the financial strength to do so may result from your decisions.

Third, do not let comparison drive your convictions. Financial considerations are important, but resist looking over the fence at how others are living and allowing that comparison to drive your decisions. Only Scripture should have that kind of influence over your decisions. Some people might make decisions that lead to great financial sacrifice and believe that's right for their goals and purposes. Others might make decisions that lead to great financial advancement and believe that's right for their goals and purposes. Both can be pleasing to the Lord! Many dangers can be avoided by focusing less on what others have or are doing and more on what God has placed in front of you to focus on.

3. Relational

Relational priorities aren't the sole drivers in a decision, but they should be considered. This could be applied to any number of relationships, and everyone's situation will be unique in various ways. Here are some potential relationships to consider:

1. Church leaders who care for us spiritually
2. Friends who are there for us
3. Family who mean so much to us

I am going to leave the list there, but you should add to it accordingly. To help shed more light on these three relational priorities, let me break down how they can be considered. Church leaders are not God, nor are they permitted to lord their authority over church members (1 Peter 5:1–3), but they are given spiritual care of believers and, when qualified, provide valuable spiritual oversight and wisdom (Heb. 13:17).

Is your decision to move to another state going to include healthy church leadership? Will you be consulting a church leader for prayer, guidance, and wisdom? Are there church leaders who know your strengths and weaknesses and can give guidance to your new church leaders elsewhere? Have you considered the way that your relationships with church leaders can affect your home, maturity, and overall spiritual health? My advice: Don't make a major move without planning and prioritizing a relationship with church leaders who will care for you. Jesus never intended for his sheep to wander without undershepherds to care for them.

Friends are another relational priority that should be considered because friendships are an integral part of the Christian life. The Bible makes a big deal about friendships that sharpen us, challenge us, and push us to walk in the truth (Prov. 27:6, 17). I was recently watching a documentary about Jackie Robinson, the first black Major League Baseball player who broke the color barrier and numerous other barriers in the late 1940s and '50s. Many people were so viciously racist during that era and few looked kindly on the Brooklyn Dodgers signing Jackie Robinson. He had to deal with racial slurs, threats on and off the field, and the constant humiliation that crowds forced him to endure.

During one game a white teammate named Pee Wee Reese walked over to Jackie and put his arm around him, then turned to face the crowd, making it clear that he was Jackie's friend and would not allow their racial prejudice to dictate his friendship with Jackie. Later on, as the story goes, Jackie

Robinson said it was the arm of Pee Wee Reese wrapped around his shoulder that saved his life. Good friendships are like that, and they are hard to find. You can make more money and not find true friendship. You can have a bigger house for a cheaper price and not find true friendship. You can live in the city of your dreams or in a countryside villa but still not find true friendship. Friendship is one of life's vital organs and great gifts from God. Many times, it will be the priority of meaningful friendships that help us make—or not make—decisions.

Finally, family relationships can be a major factor in our decision-making priorities. The way you define family relationships can vary, but they generally include your spouse, kids, grandkids, parents, siblings, and extended family as well. When you give these relationships proper thought, you can make decisions effectively and with confidence, knowing you have considered the people whom you love before reaching a conclusion about what you will do.

4. Eternal

This is without question the most important priority to factor into every decision you make. How will what you do affect eternity? The British missionary to China C. T. Studd had this priority in mind when he wrote, "Only one life 'twill soon be past. Only what's done for Christ will last." We are by nature shortsighted people, but God has called us to be eternally minded people. In Philippians 3, Paul is unpacking the overall goal of his life, and can you guess what is front and center in his mind? Philippians 3:7 captures the entire thought in some of the most eternally focused language in all his letters: "But whatever things were gain to me, those things I have counted as loss for the sake of Christ" (NASB 1995). Later in the chapter he goes on to say, "I press on toward the goal for the prize of the upward call of God in Christ Jesus" (v. 14).

In Paul's eyes nothing mattered more than eternity. He had been a big-time religious leader, he knew the Law, he had been so confident in his religious elitism, he was from the tribe of Benjamin (a big deal!), and he was a "Hebrew of Hebrews" (Phil. 3:5). Yet by the time he writes this epistle from prison, he has come to be held captive by Christ and his calling to preach, suffer, and live all out for the gospel.

As you consider your course in life and seek God's will in your decision-making process, where does pressing on toward the goal come into play? Not merely your goals but *the* goal? As Christians, God has saved us not so that we may live a life full of pleasure for ourselves but rather so that we may live a life full of purpose for him. Is there fun to be had? Memories to be made? Enjoyment to fill our hearts? And even satisfaction to be experienced? Of course! God is a loving Father who lavishes grace, freedom, joy, creativity, and pleasure upon us. We were made to enjoy God and bring him glory through our lives—that includes enjoying the good gifts he provides here on earth. But in all of these things there really is only one thing we're living for: eternity. A Christian is never without an eternal perspective.

5. Has God Given Us Permission?

Based on what the Bible teaches, I believe we have more freedom in our decision-making than we often think. Unless a decision is accompanied by an explicit sin, the Bible paints a bigger-picture mentality wherein glorifying God is the ultimate goal. This is liberating for people who have anxiety over every microdecision they make. I know believers who are superstitious over every little decision, imagining that they could lose God's favor and blessing with any trivial decision. This crippling trap comes from a sneaky form of legalism that says God is waiting to give you a divine backhand if you buy one car over the other, or move into a different house, take a different job, or even go to a different school. As a part of healthy decision-making, Christians must consider some simple but monumental questions:

- Has God spoken explicitly on this issue?
- Has God left decisions like this up to Christian liberty?
- Has God provided principles in Scripture that can inform your decision?
- Has God commanded you to do something in the midst of this decision?
- Has God commanded you to be something in the midst of this decision?

Just by asking these questions and considering the permission of God in a given decision, you will find yourself more confident and more informed than ever before.

6. Have We Considered the Long-Term Perspective?

From beginning to end, God is a planner. He planned for creation, planned for our salvation (Eph. 1:4), planned for our sanctification (Phil. 1:6), and planned for our ultimate glorification (Rom. 8:30–31). If God is a planner with a long-term perspective, we ought to imitate him as his image bearers. One of the ways we can do that is in our decision-making process. As human beings we are naturally driven by our immediate desires. Instant gratification is an ever-present temptation as we look to make decisions that satisfy daily desires. For a Christian the short-term results of any given decision are not unimportant, but they are not the primary drivers. The long-term perspective must be given its place as we think deeply, humbly, and prudently about how our decisions will affect the future.

Even as I write this, I think of decisions I should have made with long-term perspective but at the time of certain decisions I didn't have the discipline or maturity to think that way. You're likely no different and can easily think of decisions you wish you'd made with the endgame in mind. While you cannot control the past, you can control how you make decisions with the future in mind. Here are several key questions to always consider under the banner of "If the Lord wills" (James 4:15):

- Where am I likely going to be as a result of this decision in one year, five years, ten years, and twenty years?

- Is this decision rooted in short-term emotions that are blinding me from long-term perspective?
- How will this decision affect my future and the futures of my spouse and children?
- Are there other options I need to consider because they are better in the long run?
- Is this a short-term decision accompanied by tempered expectations?
- Will this decision lead to long-term spiritual growth?

These are not the only questions you should ask yourself, but they are a good start when thinking of the long-term results of any given decision. God planned ahead and had the end in mind. Imitate him!

7. Is This Decision Accompanied by Peace?

Have you ever made a decision, then experienced pushback from people only to respond with a spiritualized statement like "Well, regardless of what *you* think, I feel peace about it"? I wouldn't say it's wrong or sinful to rest in the fact that you feel a subjective peace about a decision, but I would say that's like the dessert portion of a meal. Sure, it's sweet to experience that feeling subjectively, but to make great decisions that honor God, you should also pursue an objective peace. In the end subjective peace can be misleading because your personal feelings can fool you. Meanwhile, objective peace can be revealing. Let me give you an example of objective peace.

Imagine a major decision needs to be made in your home

(assume this is a home with a husband and wife, but you can apply this to your life if you're single too). When it comes down to two options, almost all the *P*s check out except for "peace." The potential decision is causing major conflict in your marriage. You think one thing, your spouse thinks another. You pray, consult, study Scripture, and weigh all options. In the end the decision continues to cause so much conflict that you and your spouse can't find objective peace.

This lack of peace should lead to bigger questions to ask to dig deeper into the heart behind the decision:

- Why does the decision upset you? Is there a danger ahead you're concerned about?
- Do you think you are being disobedient to the Lord and your spouse is blind to it?
- Are you holding on to superficial things that are keeping you from moving forward?
- Have you taken a hasty and rushed approach to the decision and overlooked important factors?
- Have spiritual priorities been neglected in order to pursue materialistic ones?
- Is a sense of ego, idolatry, or selfishness linked to the decision?

The goal is to pursue objective peace that comes from your spouse, a trusted friend or adviser, or others. Again, you can value personal or subjective peace, but decision-making strength often comes from an abundance of counselors.

A Real-Life Example

I have a friend and beloved church member who rightfully takes church involvement seriously. He was saved under our ministry a few years ago, got baptized, and is a part of my small weekly men's Bible study. He and his wife had their first baby in our church, and they are deeply loved. One day he sat down to ask me about a potential move to another state. I could tell the conversation made him a little nervous, and he seemed concerned with getting it right. One of his first questions revealed a great deal of humility and prudence.

He said, "I just want to be honest up front. Both my wife and I know that this move is a want, not a need. We love the people here, we are thankful for all that God has done, and we'd like to move to that region of the country to buy a little acreage, raise our kids in a more outdoorsy environment, maybe have a cow, some chickens, and enjoy our life serving the Lord and raising a family." Then the big question came.

He said, "Is that sinful and the wrong motive?"

My heart was filled with compassion for this brother. I could see him wrestling with what so many Christians wrestle with. Is it a sin to move to another state and enjoy some land? Are you offending God by having a lawn to cut, chickens to feed, and a traditional environment instead of grinding it out in a suburban or city environment? Perhaps the most insecure question that lies underneath the surface is this: *Am I a bad Christian for leaving this church and going to a different one because I want to move?*

I knew what he was going through because I have seen and heard of pastors who abuse their authority when people want to move states. I have seen and heard of pastors guilt-tripping people as though they weren't the committed and strong remnant who stick around at the church. My friend might have directly or indirectly internalized some of those external expectations. Or he might have been experiencing his own internally generated guilt.

As he and I talked through the decision, the seven *P*s provided a road map for us both to consider. I asked him first and foremost whether he had prayed, and he affirmed that he had. Second, I asked him whether he had thought through his priorities, knowing that he had prudently sought counsel and was unfolding his process. His response still makes me smile to this day.

"Yes," he started. "I actually mapped out everything, and we wouldn't even be moving to this region if there wasn't a solid church nearby. We found one and believe we can prioritize our spiritual well-being in the midst of the move and for the future."

What was I to say? From there we covered his financial probabilities, employment logistics, and unity and peace between him and his wife, along with some encouraging "permissions" that we have as believers. When you've walked through the fundamentals for the fork in the road, and God is opening doors through providence along the way, then it's time to decide!

So what did they decide? Well, funny enough, with total

support and love from their church and our leaders regardless of what they chose, and even after some house-hunting in the new state, they decided to stay. When I asked the reason why they decided to stick around, he said, "We believe it's too soon and don't want to leave right now. With everything going on at the church and our relationships here, we want to keep growing and will revisit it down the road."

Friend, sometimes you'll go. Sometimes you'll stay. Sometimes you'll wait. Above all, sometimes you'll wonder. But a fork in the road does not have to be a devastating experience that steals your joy, breeds insecurity, ignites anxiety, and causes conflict. You can use these fundamentals and establish a healthy foundation for God-honoring decisions.

Learning to Live

1. Recognize that great decisions are made through a process. Have you ever parked somewhere you knew you weren't supposed to? I have. Some of life's most trivial moments can turn into some of life's bigger lessons. For me, one particular moment went on to become an infamous lesson in our marriage. My wife, the rule follower, specifically warned me that our apartment complex at the time was very particular about even the slightest parking violation. If the car was even an inch into the red-colored curb (the red meant no parking), they would tow.

Parking there was hard to come by, and if you didn't

get a good spot, you'd be stuck walking an extremely long distance. Well, you can imagine what I did one day when I had to stop at home for an hour, then head back out. I saw a spot that would cause the car to be slightly in the red zone. *It's just for an hour and I am heading out again*, I said to myself, the key word being *myself*. One hour later the car was towed and I was in trouble with a $350 parking violation. We were broke newlyweds, I had been warned, and now I was going to experience pain on all fronts. Isn't that how we often make our worst mistakes? Impulse, independence, then indiscretion.

If your heart struggles to slow down and trust the process when it comes to making decisions, you likely have a pattern of impulsive decision-making that will lead to pain—if it hasn't already. Learn to love the process for how it shapes your mind and heart to be more prayerful and thoughtful about your decisions. Learn to love the good fruit of a healthy process.

2. Reject regret when you've diligently processed a decision. Are you familiar with the concept of buyer's remorse? It's when you make a purchase and immediately second-guess your decision. Sometimes regret is a necessary feeling because our decisions end up costing us more than we'd considered. But it can also result from a lack of patience and a lack of healthy process when making a decision.

For example, when I moved to Arizona and endured various trials, there was not a moment when I thought we made a mistake and should have stayed in California, because

I knew we went through a healthy and transparent process when making that decision. I *knew* it was wise and right. There were no regrets, no second-guesses, and no "shoulda, coulda, woulda."

I was recently discussing this with a seminary friend who was talking about the importance of honesty with motives and desires when he said, "We need to be as honest as possible so we can have the most honest and rigorous discussions with our wise counselors." He was pressing on the fact that if we aren't honest in the process in order to manipulate outcomes and end up where we are trying to get to, then if things get hard, we will wonder whether God is disciplining our sinful decision, as a loving Father would (Heb. 12:6), or we will second-guess whether it's all unraveling because we had deceptive motives. Can God work through our sinful decisions and turn things around? Of course. But will our confidence erode when we don't go through a prudent process? I believe so.

When you've gone through a biblical process for making decisions, you can reject the regret that comes in the aftermath. When you've stuck to a process, prayed, exercised prudence, assessed priorities, studied God's permission, maintained eternal perspective, and experienced objective peace, you can rest assured that regret has no place in your life, even through trials or when things don't go the way you had planned. Move forward with confidence no matter what comes and trust that God's will is unfolding for your good and his glory (Rom. 8:28).

3. Resolve to be humble with each step. In recent years I have sat with my fair share of individuals who were dead set on a decision before ever seeking counsel. Not long ago a man came into my office to make a decision that would affect his employment, his living situation, his portfolio, his marriage, and his future. When I asked him how we could be of service or whether he needed counsel from me or any of our elders, he said, "Oh, no thanks! We already made up our minds but just wanted to let you know since you're our pastor." I prayed for them, the meeting ended, and they've been spinning in chaos ever since.

Our elders never demand that people ask for pastoral wisdom or seek counsel before making an important decision, but it's always saddening to see how high the pain rates are for people who make up their minds in a vacuum. I'm all for people exercising independent thinking when it comes to living everyday life, living for Christ, and not listening to world or peer pressure to compromise on the truth, but when it comes to making major life decisions or entertaining ideas that will lead to monumental changes, words like *community*, *dependence*, *counsel*, and *informed* are lifelines.

I bet if you review the past five, ten, or even fifteen years of your life, you could identify a lack of humility as a root cause of bad decisions. A lack of humility can be seen in your ego driving you into impulsive decisions or your pride causing you to reject wise counsel from others who told you, "Slow down and think through this decision!" Humility is a gift from the Lord we often reject. Proverbs 19:20 is the perfect reminder, saying, "Listen to counsel and accept discipline, that you may be wise the rest of your days" (NASB 1995). You cannot experience longevity as a great decision-maker if you are not humble and don't listen to wise counsel.

Questions for Reflection and Discussion

1. Think of a bad decision you've made in the past few years. Which *P* would have saved you a lot of headaches?
2. Why is it important to take all the *P*s into consideration and not rush into decisions?
3. Impure motives can deceive us into thinking a decision is wise when it is foolish. How do you guard against this?
4. List three or four people you can go to for wise counsel and why each would be someone you could glean wisdom from.
5. Make a list of your top five priorities in life and use these the next time you make an important decision.

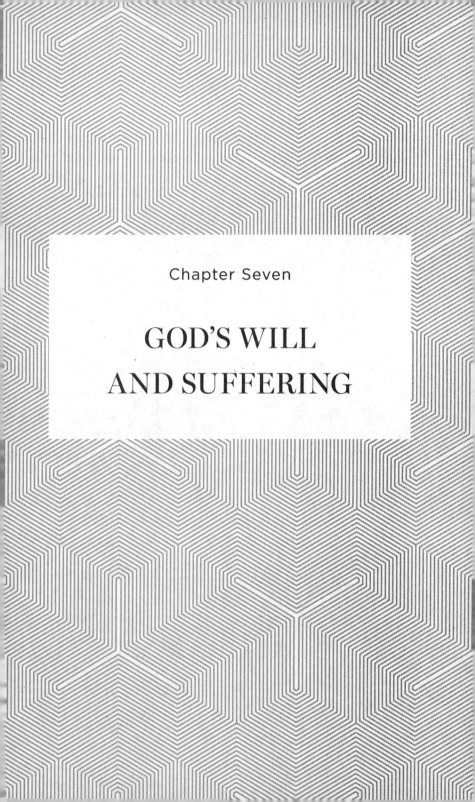

Chapter Seven

GOD'S WILL
AND SUFFERING

Until around the age of twenty-six, I did not have an accurate view of suffering and how it relates to God's will. I used to see someone in dire straits and immediately think, "Hmm, that's so sad for them," without ever once thinking their unfortunate circumstance could ever happen to me. Life and, of course, the Lord Jesus have a way of teaching you sooner than later that in this world you will have trouble (John 16:33). Real life eventually hits all of us, no matter who you are. A childhood cancer diagnosis with our three-month-old son back in 2018, family conflict over the gospel, financial struggles, multiple jobs to make ends meet, multiple miscarriages, and more—there's no escaping the troubles and trials of life.

Before truth transformed my life, I dogmatically believed that I could speak health, wealth, and happiness into reality. People today call this "manifesting," and it's incredibly popular in motivational speaking and entrepreneurial circles. In my opinion suffering was only a sign of God's disapproval. If someone was suffering, I assumed they had done something to invite it and needed to fix their behavior immediately; then, and only then, God would relent and bless them once again.

In a very callous and prideful way, I believed that if you had enough faith, did all the right things, gave lots of money to the church, and declared positive things, you could live a life devoid of sickness and suffering. If you're familiar with my testimony, you know how the true gospel changed my life; if not, you may benefit from my book *God, Greed, and the (Prosperity) Gospel.*

While you may not hold to the so-called prosperity gospel, or believe the extreme things I did, we all tend to have an oversimplified theology of suffering that looks like this equation:

Faith in Jesus for salvation
+ Good works for God
= A blessed life

This view leads to frustration when things get hard and we suffer because we assume—even in our ignorance—that life goes well for those who do good. Our attitude when we suffer reveals that we believed it to be God's will to give us a good life if we do morally good things. The core of this mentality is not biblical truth but works-based moralism and entitlement. Nowhere in Scripture does God guarantee smooth sailing if you follow him. God doesn't always define the "blessed life" the way we do.

Sure, he will bless obedience. He will bless faithfulness. And, yes, there *might* be some material benefits at your job or in your relationships when you operate with wisdom according to God's will. But none of your good deeds guarantee that you will not suffer. The Bible teaches the precise opposite when we live for Christ. But we do well to define blessings, suffering, and his will the way Scripture does, and reject what ear-tickling false teachers say to lure in the masses for a shady payday.

Sometimes we act like the disciples in John 9 when they came upon a blind man and asked Jesus, "Rabbi, who sinned, this man or his parents, that he would be born blind?" (v. 2). The Jews had preconceived notions that tied the sin of a parent to the sickness or suffering of a child. Jesus corrected his disciples' broad-brush theological view by saying, "It was neither that this man sinned, nor his parents; but it was so that the works of God might be displayed in him" (v. 3). Notice that Jesus didn't rebuke their reasoning completely, but he corrected their misapplication. The Bible does teach that poor decisions and sin can lead to self-inflicted consequences that involve suffering, sickness, and even death (1 Cor. 11:30), but none of these truths are held in a vacuum; they are part of a healthy and holistic theology of suffering.

I have written a book on suffering and enduring trials by keeping your eyes on Jesus that covers this topic in greater depth. The book is titled *More Than a Healer* and would be a blessing to anyone wondering how to navigate the storms of life. But for now I want to provide you with wisdom from God's Word that will enable you to trust him when you make mistakes, when decisions don't turn out the way you expected, or when you've done everything right but things still go wrong. When you are tempted to despair and give up, these truths will give you comfort and confidence. They are truths about God, about suffering, and about the way God has willed you and me to suffer for the name of Christ, and they will help you go forward stronger and with more clarity than ever.

Truths about God

When we suffer in life, we always want to start with truths about God, because the more we know God, the more stable we are when the unpredictable happens. He is our anchor in the storm. What we know about God will direct our course. Just as a compass guides an aviator through thick fog, our knowledge of God will give us spiritual clarity when our emotions cloud our judgment.

Truth 1: God Is Sovereign over Everything

That God is sovereign means that he is supreme and rules over all. There isn't a ray of sunshine, a raindrop, or a single speck of sand that operates outside his authority. (As noted before, his authority includes both his explicit and permitted will.) Everything is under his power. If God is not sovereign, he is not God. Believing that God is in control even when we are suffering can come off as crazy to many people in our world today, but that's because it's a supernatural way of thinking, more suited to life in another kingdom—God's.

Truth 2: God Is Good Even When Things Are Not

One of the most detrimental things to us as we walk in God's will is a wrong view of God's character—his goodness in particular. Many people will naturally assume they are out of God's will because they are enduring a trial, believing that they can't be in God's will because God is always good

196

and things are always good when we are in his will. This is the result of deficient teaching, but the Bible helps us see the truth.

God is good all the time, not because our circumstances are good, but because his character is good. All throughout the Bible, God's people are shown encountering both immensely good times and horribly hard times. Yet through it all the Bible itself declares God's goodness. The Psalms are filled with declarations of God's goodness composed by David even when he was going through pain. While enduring King Saul's jealous rage and attempts to kill him (1 Sam. 18:11; 19:10), experiencing injustices and betrayals (1 Sam. 23:15–29), waiting years to take his rightful place as king, and running like a fugitive from his own rebellious and tyrannical son (2 Sam. 15:13–17:22), David still declared the goodness of God. Psalm 106:1 exalts God, exclaiming, "Praise the LORD. Give thanks to the LORD, for he is good; his love endures forever" (NIV). Psalm 107:1 repeats nearly the same words and so do Psalm 118:1 and Psalm 136:1. The theme of thanksgiving is prevalent in these praises, which reminds us again that we can praise God in the midst of pain. He is good, even when our circumstances are not!

Truth 3: God Works All Things for His Glory and Your Good

Romans 8:28 is a commonly quoted passage, but it's easily misunderstood. Paul writes, "And we know that for those who love God all things work together for good, for those

who are called according to his purpose" (ESV). People sometimes assume this passage means that everything is going to
be good and God has willed for you to enjoy health, wealth,
and happiness no matter what decisions you make. I've heard
countless prosperity preachers tell their listeners, "Wherever
you go, and whatever you decide, if you have faith, God will
bless you and work all things for your good! You just need
to declare his favor upon your life. Speak it by faith. There is
power in that declaration."

This sounds amazing, until the bottom falls out and decisions don't unfold the way you declared, or all the positive
thinking you employed doesn't stop bad things from happening to you. Rest assured, if you are a genuine follower of
Christ and believe the true (and only) gospel, God *is* working
all things for his glory and your good, but the path according
to his plan may involve trials that grow you spiritually, not
physical possessions that grow you materially.

So what does Romans 8:28 mean and how does understanding it fit into our growing closer to Jesus? First, it is
speaking specifically about "those who love God" and those
"who are called according to his purpose." These phrases are
directly aimed at genuine believers in Jesus Christ, which
means this is not a general promise you can throw around at
people like a prosperity gospel preacher telling a crowd that
God will make them happy, healthy, and wealthy. Second, this
passage says "all things," which means that the good, the bad,
and the ugly *are* going to happen. No one is immune to the
"all things" in life. Third, this passage reminds us that God's

definition of good is what will ultimately be accomplished, and his good will be good for us.

Truth 4: God Displays His Power through Our Weakness

Weakness is your friend. Shocking as it may sound, your weakness is right where you need it to be for you to see God's power put on display. A good number of years ago now, I began studying church history, and as I did, one of the most remarkable themes that emerged was how God used weak people to accomplish great things.

Wherever I found weakness, I found power. From the disciples themselves, who weren't exactly the pick of the litter; to the martyrs in the early church; to reformers such as John Knox, who wept in fear over preaching; to Spurgeon, who battled depression; to missionaries who were sickly, unlikely heroes; to individuals such as Joni Eareckson Tada, who has done more bound to a wheelchair than some could do with multiple lifetimes, God loves to use our weaknesses and put his power on display through them.

If you're suffering, rather than question God's will or doubt his goodness, embrace this truth that trumps your feelings.

Truths about Suffering

With all of that said, God will use suffering to bring about several practical outcomes. The following truths are biblical and should never be glossed over if we're to build a strong and balanced theology of suffering. Remember that we do not isolate these truths and blanket every situation with them, but rather we keep them in our theological framework to bring balance and clarity when we face times of suffering.

Truth 1: Suffering Promotes Our Sanctification

Defeats, challenges, and the valleys of life purify and purge our lives in ways that victory, ease, and mountain-peak moments never could. God will use suffering to make us holier, more dependent on him, and more aware of how much we need him. We may not love the process, but we will love the results. Again, this doesn't mean that God necessarily causes our suffering. It means that he uses it for his good purposes.

Truth 2: Suffering Inspires Our Submission

Suffering reminds us that we are not in control. We can live in a beautiful neighborhood, make great money, and have the metrics of success by earthly standards present in our lives, but nothing can form a hedge of protection that keeps suffering from entering when God sovereignly allows it to.

Perhaps you've experienced the frustration of suffering only to begin "fighting" with God in your prayers and with your attitude. You think, *God, I have done everything you've asked of me, and yet you still allow me to suffer?* After working through the normal emotions that can overtake even the strongest Christian from time to time, you will eventually submit and come to rely on God all the more.

Truth 3: Suffering Builds Our Strength

One of the best passages to help us understand God's will and our suffering comes straight from the book of Romans. Paul emphasizes the gospel through justification by faith, showing how the peace of God can be ours. He goes on to explain that we can rejoice in our sufferings for very good reason. Romans 5:1–5 says, "Therefore, having been justified by faith, we have peace with God through our Lord Jesus Christ, through whom also we have obtained our introduction by faith into this grace in which we stand; and we exult in hope of the glory of God. And not only this, but we also exult in our tribulations, knowing that tribulation brings about perseverance; and perseverance, proven character; and proven character, hope; and hope does not disappoint, because the love of God has been poured out within our hearts through the Holy Spirit who was given to us" (NASB 1995).

There is some truth to the axiom "What doesn't kill you makes you stronger," but it's most evident in the Christian who sees their character grow stronger through suffering. God's will is that we pass the heart test, though we all fail in some ways, whether it be in our attitude or in a brief moment of frustration. In the end suffering elevates our hope because we see how the love of God not only saves us but also preserves us day by day.

Truth 4: Suffering Sharpens Our Sight

Suffering here on earth accomplishes something remarkable according to the will of God—it makes us long for our eternal home and fellowship with Christ forever. In 2 Corinthians 4:16–18, Paul is finishing off a section about getting to share the gospel and experience the honor of suffering for following Christ. Instead of complaining about his lackluster retirement account or how all his imprisonments are keeping him from taking that dream vacation, he proclaims the glory of his suffering and how it is evoking in him a deeper longing than any earthly prosperity ever could: "Therefore we do not lose heart, but though our outer man is decaying, yet our inner man is being renewed day by day. For momentary, light affliction is producing for us an eternal weight of glory far beyond all comparison, while we look not at the things which are seen, but at the things which are not seen; for the things which are seen are temporal, but the things which are not seen are eternal" (NASB 1995).

Paul doesn't get down in the dumps. He doesn't lose heart like a boxer who has taken one too many blows and no longer has the will to go another round. Paul is ready for whatever the next day will bring him as long as he can serve Christ once more. With each passing day even suffering has become a sobering reminder that the unseen realm grows closer with each moment. The temporal no longer motivates him. He has traded the physical for the spiritual and the fading glory of this world for the everlasting glory of heaven. He's living for the gospel of Jesus Christ so that others can come to saving faith, and suffering only sharpens his vision of that day when his own faith will be made sight.

Scripture is abundantly clear about God's character and

about the nature of suffering and what it accomplishes in the believer. But we also need to consider truths about ourselves. How should we act when God's will allows suffering? What should our response be if we suffer unjustly for the name of Christ, as Paul did? Is it really God's will for us to suffer and, if we do, to react a certain way?

The plain truth is this: God's will is for our suffering to reflect Christ, because he suffered too.

Suffering like a Saint

I've titled this final section "Suffering like a Saint" (a saint is what the Bible calls a redeemed person) because it's not just understanding the "what" of suffering that matters, it is understanding the "way" of suffering. There is a way in which a Christian is called to suffer. One can have right doctrine on suffering but still not engage in right actions when suffering. Orthodoxy must always move to orthopraxy. To help you grasp this, I want to unpack 1 Peter 4:12–16, but first let me set the stage by taking you back in time to the life of one of my favorite missionaries.

Adoniram Judson, whom I have already introduced to you in this book, was in my opinion like a married version of the apostle Paul. During his time in the mission field, he crossed paths with malaria, dysentery, cholera, and death. He was a man whose life was filled with tragedy after tragedy, yet atop that he suffered for his faith. Losing two wives and seven of his thirteen children, watching colleagues die on the mission field, and spending his life for the cause of the gospel, Judson would eventually find himself hanging nearly upside down in the worst of prison conditions Burma had to offer.

His precious translation of the New Testament into the Burmese language—something he gave his life to—was nearly lost, and his whole life could have seemed like a wasted failure to the modern American who dreams of a pretty house, a steady 9:00 a.m. to 5:00 p.m. job with good benefits and vacations, two and a half kids, and a dog.

In contrast to the dream we likely pray to realize, Judson's reality included deep suffering, and all of that suffering led to the Word of God going forth to a people who owe their modern-day Burmese Bibles to his missionary work. In human terms, he endured a brutal life filled with crushing challenges. And yet, in all of that suffering, Judson never lost his faith, his character, or his love for Christ. The context and content of suffering may vary, but like Judson's, our character in suffering must not. We are followers of Christ not only in that we suffer but also in how we suffer.

As we discern the will of God in our lives, we should open ourselves to the reality that God may will suffering in our lives for purposes that change the world for eternity. To the flesh that kind of claim seems crazy (and dreadful). But to the spirit (what 2 Corinthians 4:16 calls "the inner man") it is glorious truth because we could only be so privileged to have our lives used for God's eternal purposes.

Persecution That God's Will Permits

In 1 Peter we read the following:

> Beloved, do not be surprised at the fiery ordeal among you,
> which comes upon you for your testing, as though some
> strange thing were happening to you; but to the degree
> that you share the sufferings of Christ, keep on rejoicing,
> so that also at the revelation of His glory you may rejoice
> with exultation. If you are reviled for the name of Christ,
> you are blessed, because the Spirit of glory and of God
> rests on you. Make sure that none of you suffers as a mur-
> derer, or thief, or evildoer, or a troublesome meddler; but
> if anyone suffers as a Christian, he is not to be ashamed,
> but is to glorify God in this name.
>
> —1 Peter 4:12–16 NASB 1995

The best evidence suggests that 1 Peter was written just
before or after the burning of Rome in AD 64. The text provides potential clues to this time frame, such as Peter's use
of the phrase "fiery trial" to describe a test that, "when it
comes," would be cause for suffering well in Christ's name
(1 Peter 4:12–13 ESV). He also tells his readers to be subject to
authority, then goes even farther, saying to "honor everyone,"
even "the emperor" (2:13–17 ESV).

While Peter makes no specific mention of the fire in Rome
during that era, it is conceivable that he is writing pertinent
truth for Christians who are going to suffering according to

the will of God. He writes from "Babylon" (a name used for Rome in New Testament writings), aware of the situation coming upon Christians, and prepares all saints, Jew and Gentile alike, for the persecution coming in their regions.

Whether merely coincidental or prophetic, the language in the letter sets the stage for a Christian's perspective in the midst of trial. When the emperor Nero needed a scapegoat for the fire he started, he blamed Christians, whom the Romans already hated and associated with Jews. Thus persecution of Christians spread out from the epicenter of Rome to the surrounding regions, including Pontus, Galatia, Cappadocia, Asia, and Bithynia.

The Roman historian Tacitus writes that Christians were so hated and persecuted that they were covered with the skins of beasts so that wild dogs would attack them, were nailed to crosses, and were used as human torches throughout the streets of Rome and in Emperor Nero's gardens. This is the world Christians found themselves in. Yet the driving theme in Peter's letter is that this world is not our home. We are citizens here but ultimately citizens of heaven. We are temporary resident aliens, put here to be witnesses for Christ, and then to be with Christ. It's all about him!

This passage contains four primary truths that I will unpack for you here.

1. Saints are not shocked by suffering for Christ.
2. Saints rejoice when suffering for Christ.

3. Saints are still sure when suffering for Christ.
4. Saints have no shame when suffering for Christ.

Each of these truths will help you understand how suffering can be attached to God's will and that God has not left us without a road map for such a challenging path.

1. Saints Are Not Shocked by Suffering for Christ

> Beloved, do not be surprised at the fiery ordeal among you, which comes upon you for your testing, as though something strange were happening to you. (1 Peter 4:12)

Why does Peter tell them this? Well, these Christians were mostly Gentile converts who were used to being in the cultural majority. In their day, Jews were used to being looked down upon, so that wouldn't be shocking. Outsiders were reviled and persecuted, so that was not news either! But for insiders to suffer would be far less common. For these native Gentiles, suffering would have come as a bit of a shock. But now they needed to embrace the fact that their new Christian identity made them a cultural minority.

America has undergone such a drastic change in worldview over the past forty years that we can relate a lot more to this now than we ever could have in generations past. (It's worth noting that most of us can't relate to their persecution.) Christians used to be in the majority of a God-believing nation that generally speaking had a moral compass that pointed more north than it does now, and today we find ourselves being Christians in a society that mirrors the wickedness described in the darkest eras of the Bible. In Peter's day he saw the total rejection of God's commands being outright celebrated. Today we see the same. The Christians throughout Asia Minor receiving 1 Peter as a letter were a cultural minority because of their faith, and so are you!

Peter refers to a "fiery ordeal" among them, and this could very well be the fire that Nero set in his drunken stupor as he burned down his own city and blamed Christians. Or, as some have argued, Peter is giving a picture of how trials are like a refining fire that tests and purifies, much like Job 23:10 describes when Job says, "When he has tested me, I will come forth as gold" (NIV). Whatever their reality in that season, suffering was a test that would prove their faith, and suffering was normal because of their faith. This is all part of God's will.

Suffering is what most of the biblical writers prepared their audiences for. First John 3:13 says, "Do not be surprised, brothers, that the world hates you" (ESV). And right about here is where I could rip on prosperity gospel preachers, and people who believe the prosperity gospel, too, but we should look in the mirror and think about the last time we leaned into one of these mindsets:

- *Maybe I should've done more to please God and he wouldn't have let me get cancer.*

- *If I had given more money to the church, my kids would have been saved. I should have sowed that seed after all.*
- *If I obey God and am moral and conservative and vote right and go to church, I will be blessed.*
- *Why are they treating us Christians this way? Don't they know we're a Christian nation?*

The kinds of attitudes I have described do not capture the essence of a balanced Christian worldview. We need to stop being shocked when we suffer for Christ. Our identity as Christians makes us a cultural minority.

Instead of being shocked, we should rejoice!

2. Saints Rejoice When Suffering for Christ

To the degree that you share the sufferings of Christ, keep on rejoicing, so that also at the revelation of His glory you may rejoice with exultation. (1 Peter 4:13 NASB 1995)

The word for *rejoicing* here is a Greek word that describes being in a state of happiness, which means you may be enduring pain but you haven't lost your perspective. You may be suffering for your faith but you still know that God is faithful. And don't miss the anchor for the soul here in Peter's statement when he highlights that they are sharing in the sufferings of Christ. This is the truth! Their suffering is identification with Christ, not in a salvific sense but in a

WALKING *in* GOD'S WILL

relational one. As believers we joyfully identify with Christ, and that includes in his sufferings.

Action with Christ	Reference
Crucified together	Galatians 2:20
Dead together	Colossians 2:20
Buried together	Romans 6:4
Alive together	Ephesians 2:5
Raised together	Colossians 3:1
Suffering together	Romans 8:17
Glorified together	Romans 8:17

We identify with all of Christ, and as his followers we will be like Christ. Paul invites Timothy into the normal reality of suffering for Jesus, writing in 2 Timothy 2:3, "Suffer hardship with me, as a good soldier of Christ Jesus." Faithful saints suffer and consider it a joy to identify with Christ in this way. Philippians 1:29 goes even farther, saying it's God's will for believers to suffer and it's actually a privilege! Paul adds, "For to you it has been granted for Christ's sake, not only to believe in Him, but also to suffer for His sake" (NASB 1995).

The joy in suffering for saints is that we are suffering because of allegiance to Christ. It is joy! Even a privilege! Although this mindset does not necessarily ease the pain, it can give purpose as we seek God's will. We can say, "I rejoice because in this suffering I am just like my Lord!"

And to that truth some will inevitably say, "I don't want to follow after Jesus in his suffering!" In reply to such a statement, it must be asked, "Then do you even follow him at all?" The Jesus of Christianity is not a "safe" Christ. He was a suffering one. The glory is not in this life but in the life to come.

To drive that truth home, Peter reinforces that they "keep on rejoicing, so that also at the revelation of His glory you may rejoice with exultation." There is an eschatological promise here with joy attached to what is coming. These Christians aren't living their best lives now, they are living for a life to come! When you share in the sufferings of Christ and rejoice and remain faithful, you have evidence that you belong to him. And that only increases your joy and longing for the day when those who suffer for him will be glorified with him. Colossians 3:3–4 says, "For you have died, and your life is hidden with Christ in God. When Christ, who is our life, is revealed, then you also will be revealed with Him in glory." We rejoice at the privilege to share in his suffering.

Acts 5:41–42 showcases the aftermath of the apostles being flogged, then ordered not to speak in the name of Jesus: "So they went on their way from the presence of the Council, rejoicing that they had been considered worthy to suffer shame for His name. And every day, in the temple and from house to house, they kept right on teaching and preaching Jesus as the Christ" (NASB 1995). They were, as Thomas Watson once wrote, "graced to be disgraced for Christ."[1]

We don't glory in the pain in some sadistic way as though the pain were the goal. It's not a competition to see who can have it worse for Jesus; rather, we rejoice because we draw close to him when we are like him. We rejoice because we know that God has a purpose for our suffering, just as he did for his Son's suffering. We rejoice knowing that God does his best work during some of the most brutal moments of our lives, which gives us confidence that we can walk in his will even during difficulty.

3. Saints Are Still Sure When Suffering for Christ

> If you are reviled for the name of Christ, you are blessed, because the Spirit of glory and of God rests on you. (1 Peter 4:14 NASB 1995)

God's will is not that you wallow in confusion or insecurity when you suffer but that you remain sure without a shadow of a doubt that you are his child and in his will. That is what Peter is getting at here. The word *revile* paints the picture of heaping loads of insults and shame on someone. These insults and mockery are not merited or true, yet you are blessed when these slanderous insults are hurled your way. My mind echoes with Matthew 5:11 here, when Jesus says, "Blessed are you when people insult you and persecute you, and falsely say all kinds of evil against you because of Me."

Think about this and how it relates to your life. Here is why a believer in this situation can be sure of God's will when suffering for Christ:

1. Faithfulness *to* Christ brought this suffering.
2. A reputation *like* Christ's brought this suffering.
3. Boldness *for* Christ brought this suffering.

To suffer for these reasons can only mean that you are right where God has called you to be. You have no need to be insecure; you can be sure. He who has called you is faithful (1 Thess. 5:24). Peter's statement that "the Spirit of glory and of God rests on you" speaks of three things:

1. *God's favor.* While you are reviled by this world, you have been redeemed by God. That's his favor on you.
2. *God's promise.* While you have been persecuted by this world, you have been given the Holy Spirit as a pledge by God (Eph. 1:13–14). That's his promise.
3. *God's presence.* While this world pushes you out, his presence draws you in. Whatever you are called because of your faithfulness to Christ, God calls you the temple of the Holy Spirit, and he dwells in you!

Corrie ten Boom once said, "To realize the worth of the anchor, we need to feel the stress of the storm." When you suffer for Christ and the waves of trial crash against your life, you will be sure when you are in Christ. All hell can come against you, but your confidence won't be shaken. All can abandon you, but you won't be alone. All can be lost, but when you have Christ, you have everything you need.

In all of these things, there is a warning and one final affirmation we need to consider.

4. Saints Have No Shame When Suffering for Christ

> Make sure that none of you suffers as a murderer, or thief, or evildoer, or a troublesome meddler; but if anyone suffers as a Christian, he is not to be ashamed, but is to glorify God in this name. (1 Peter 4:15–16)

There is a vast difference between suffering through trials that come upon us and suffering through self-inflicted consequences. The Bible says to "rejoice" in trials, so a trial isn't caused by your sin; otherwise the Bible would say, "Repent!"

Now, upon first glance, "murderer, or thief, or evildoer" might cause us to tune out. That's not many of us, Peter! But he doesn't stop there. He adds in the "troublesome meddler." This is the busybody, the person who meddles in the affairs of others and ends up suffering for it. This is invasive, tasteless, and petty behavior. This is you acting ungodly, reviling revilers, fighting evil with evil, not living on mission, and forgetting that Christians do not use carnal means or attitudes to build the kingdom of God. Peter is saying that suffering like a saint means we don't behave unsaintly. Wisdom, resolve, balance, courage, conviction, prudence, and a loving gentleness are still to be present when we suffer.

Many Christians ask for trouble when they operate like

rioting zealots, calling such behavior "evangelism" or "standing for Christ." It's not standing for Christ if you don't act like Christ. Take the person who is doing ninety-five miles per hour on the freeway, gets a ticket, then says that the cop is just persecuting them because they have a cross on their bumper. No! You broke the law!

Could it be that some of us need to look at ourselves in the mirror and get honest, saying, "It's time to wake up!" That what we are going through may not be a trial but a consequence? Take seriously the words "If anyone suffers as a Christian, he is not to be ashamed, but is to glorify God in this name" and discern whether that's you. This passage paints a picture of someone who is shamed by the world for living out their faith so boldly, but who will be rewarded by God. This is the confident Christian who knows whom they belong to, why they are here, and whom they answer to. "Glorify God in this name" likely refers to being called a Christian.

Do you glory in the one you follow? Do you rejoice in suffering because you are like your Lord? Do you embrace all that comes at you on this earth as if you are living for heaven?

Do not be shocked. Suffering is normal. Rejoice and be confident. For even if the whole world turns on you, if God is for you, who can be against you?

God's will is that you take his word to heart, walk in obedience, live boldly for Christ, repent when you sin, trust his grace day by day, and believe that he is working all things together for your good and his ultimate glory (Rom. 8:28).

Learning to Live

1. Get honest about suffering versus self-inflicted consequences. Many times we jump to the conclusion that something is a trial and we define it as suffering, when it's actually a self-inflicted consequence. One of the best ways to walk in God's will is to get honest about why you're in the situation you're in. The sooner you get honest, the sooner you will find joy and peace to remain or course correct.

2. Guard your heart when things don't go your way. One of the best applications of our passage from 1 Peter is that God has made his will clear about how we should endure suffering and navigate challenges. Even when all hell breaks loose, we don't have any grounds for acting like the devil. In the beginning and still today Lucifer opposes God, slanders God, and turns his back on God. Guard your heart against bitterness when God's will unfolds differently than you expected.

3. Know that God's grace is greater than your greatest mistakes. I believe that God is so powerful, so in control, and so gracious that your greatest mistakes cannot shock him or shake him. His grace is unmerited favor upon you. Therefore, grace means that his will is always unfolding, whether you have nailed it or not, made the perfect decision or not, or reaped the bitter results of decisions you regret, and his grace can cover the mistakes you and I make in our weakness and sin.

It's not about perfection, it's about progression. Keep seeking God and, by grace, walking in his will.

Questions for Reflection and Discussion

1. How do you discern the difference between genuine suffering according to God's will and self-inflicted consequences?

2. Think back to some of your biggest mistakes and bad decisions. How has God's grace worked in spite of those mistakes, and what lessons did you learn?

3. When was the last time you suffered some kind of loss or challenge for taking a stand for Christ? What was hard about it? What was encouraging?

4. What would you tell someone who believed that it was never God's will for any of us to suffer?

5. List some of the most valuable takeaways from this book that helped you understand what it means to walk in God's will.

ENCOURAGEMENT FOR THE ROAD AHEAD

In 2005 the Smithsonian received a very intriguing donation from a merchant seaman named Waldemar Semenov. He donated a compass with a backstory for the history books. During World War II, he was serving on an American merchant ship called SS *Alcoa Guide*. On the night of April 16, 1942, a German submarine opened fire on the merchant ship, which had no guns or escort ships for protection. The ship caught fire and began to sink a few hundred miles off the coast of North Carolina.

As someone who had seen combat scenarios before, Semenov stayed calm and immediately went down to his cabin to put on a new suit, then headed to the galley for a few extra loaves of bread, since he knew they would be at sea for a while. Then he and the rest of the crew all climbed off the ship and into lifeboats. Reports confirm that the Germans did not fire on the small boats because, "in those days, everyone played by the rules," noted Semenov.

Even though they were alive, the men in the lifeboats were not out of the danger zone by any stretch. But using the small compass on the lifeboat, they sailed west-by-northwest toward the shipping lanes, where—after three days—they were spotted by a patrol plane that was searching for lost sailors from any ships sunk that week. Semenov and the crew were saved by a plane—but they were also saved by a compass. Years after the event, Semenov still had the compass in his possession and graciously gave it to the museum.[1]

When I think about that story, I can't help but reflect on the compass in contrast with everything going on around it. Think of the sound of guns and bombs, the shouts of fear, the crackling flames, and the billowing smoke, along with the sounds and smells of the ocean. The sailors would have been fearful, wondering what fate awaited them in lifeboats lost at sea. And yet the compass was there. It guided their way, reminding them that there would be a destination on the other side of the journey, and that, despite their circumstances, following the compass would lead them where they needed to go.

As you reflect on all that you've read in these pages and seek to put it into action, remember the compass of God's Word and how it can be a source of comfort and direction even when things around you are uncertain. Whether you are in a season of great success or difficult suffering, you have not been left without a compass. It needs to be said: God will get you where he wants you to be, one way or another.

To encourage you forward, here are three final summary statements that you can take with you wherever your decisions lead:

1. *God is sovereign over your best and worst decisions.* Many of us have had this thought, even if we know it's not true: *Oh no! I've made a terrible mistake and ruined everything. Now everything is out of control and will never be okay.* That's precisely what the devil would love for you to believe. He specializes in tempting you to believe that your worst decisions will define you for the rest of your life and that God is unable to control where things go from here. But remember what you've read, studied, and learned. As R. C. Sproul preached time and time again, "There are no maverick molecules in the universe." God is sovereign over everything. Rest in that truth on your best day—and your worst day.

2. *God is faithful, and if he brings you to it, he will bring you through it.* We might believe God is sovereign in allowing us to be brought *to* a situation, but like Peter walking on water, we often take our eyes off Jesus and suddenly don't believe he is sovereign to bring us *through* the situation. As you navigate decisions big and small, and as you ride out the turbulence that comes with trials, always remember that the same God who allowed your challenging circumstance is the God who will end it. The

God called Alpha is also the Omega. He is the beginning and the end. He exists outside time. Nothing can bind him or liberate him. He is and forever will be the great I Am (Ex. 3:14).

3. *God is the only one who always gets it right.* If you're looking for perfection in your decisions, you'll spend your life looking for something that does not exist. You will find perfection only in God, so it's best to keep seeking him. From that place of seeking him, everything else will flow. No, you won't be perfect, but yes, you will be progressing. God will use your heart of love and obedience to keep your life going on the trajectory he wants it to go. And even when you don't get it right, don't worry, he will work it out for good if you love him and are called according to his purpose (Rom. 8:28). If your faith is anchored to the rock of Jesus Christ, you *are* that one who is called according to his purpose. Relish that promise. Go forward with confidence.

NOTES

Chapter 1: God's Will and Your Purpose

1. Francis Foulkes, *Ephesians: An Introduction and Commentary*, 2nd ed., Tyndale New Testament Commentaries 10 (Downers Grove, IL: InterVarsity Press, 1989), 154.
2. Edward Judson, *The Life of Adoniram Judson* (New York: Anson D. F. Randolph and Company, 1883), 14–15.
3. John Piper, "Don't Waste Your Life: Seven Minutes That Moved a Generation," Desiring God, May 19, 2017, www .desiringgod.org/messages/boasting-only-in-the-cross /excerpts/dont-waste-your-life#.

Chapter 2: God's Will for Every Christian

1. Gary Inrig, *A Call to Excellence* (Wheaton, IL: Victor Books, 1985), 98.
2. Elisabeth Elliot, *Discipline: The Glad Surrender* (Grand Rapids, MI: Revell, 1982), 148.
3. D. Michael Martin, *The New American Commentary: An Exegetical and Theological Exposition of Holy Scripture*, vol. 33, *1, 2 Thessalonians* (Nashville: Broadman and Holman, 1995), 181.
4. Leon Morris, *1 and 2 Thessalonians: An Introduction and Commentary*, Tyndale New Testament Commentaries 13 (Downers Grove, IL: InterVarsity Press, 1984), 104.
5. The study that uncovered this can be accessed here: www

.barna.com/research/the-state-of-the-bible-6-trends-for
-2014/#.

6. The study can be accessed here: www.barna.com/research
/2017-bible-minded-cities/.

Chapter 3: Does God Have Multiple Wills?

1. Joni Eareckson Tada, "Ten Words That Changed Everything about My Suffering," Desiring God, September 7, 2021, www.desiringgod.org/articles/ten-words-that-changed -everything-about-my-suffering.

2. I want to thank my friend and doctoral classmate Daron Roberts for his significant feedback and editorial contributions in this section. He preached a sermon on the subject of Judas's betrayal and the sovereignty of God at his church, Cornerstone Bible Church, in Katy, Texas. Our discussion stirred insights that I pray are a benefit to readers.

3. Costi Hinn, "How to Study the Bible," For the Gospel, September 28, 2024, www.forthegospel.org/read/how-to -study-the-bible.

4. John MacArthur and Richard Mayhue, eds., *Biblical Doctrine: A Systematic Summary of Bible Truth* (Wheaton, IL: Crossway, 2017), 187.

5. MacArthur and Mayhue, *Biblical Doctrine*, 187–88. For more on these two aspects of the divine will, see John Piper, "Are There Two Wills in God?" in *Still Sovereign: Contemporary Perspectives on Election, Foreknowledge, and Grace*, ed. Thomas R. Schreiner and Bruce A. Ware (Grand Rapids: Baker, 2000), 107–31.

6. John H. Sammis, "Trust and Obey" (1887).

Chapter 4: Your View of God's Word Shapes Your View of God's Will

1. For much more on the glorious person and work of the Holy Spirit, my book *Knowing the Spirit: Who He Is, What He Does, and How He Can Transform Your Christian Life* may

strengthen you and help you live the Spirit-filled life more consistently.

2. Derek Kidner, *Psalms 1–72: An Introduction and Commentary*, Tyndale Old Testament Commentaries 15 (Downers Grove, IL: InterVarsity Press, 1973), 117.

3. Austin Duncan, "Ready, Fire, Aim!" Grace Community Church, July 18, 2023, YouTube video, www.youtube.com /watch?v=qIvnf_ZDW64. This sermon is a masterful display of expository preaching and a much-needed exhortation to many people who counsel like a theological jackhammer. I've borrowed some of his thoughts with his permission.

Chapter 5: Decision-Making Cripplers
1. *Today in the Word*, Moody Bible Institute, April 1990, 41.

Chapter 6: Fundamentals for Every Fork in the Road
1. *Merriam-Webster.com Dictionary*, s.v. "prudence," accessed October 13, 2024, www.merriam-webster.com/dictionary /prudence.

Chapter 7: God's Will and Suffering
1. Thomas Watson wrote in *A Body of Divinity*, "The apostles departed from the council, 'rejoicing that they were counted worthy to suffer shame for Christ's name,' Acts 5:41: that they were graced to be disgraced for Christ."

Epilogue: Encouragement for the Road Ahead
1. Owen Edwards, "A Compass Saves the Crew," *Smithsonian*, September 2009, www.smithsonianmag.com/smithsonian -institution/a-compass-saves-the-crew-40699276/.

ONLINE RESOURCES FROM COSTI W. HINN

Costi W. Hinn (@costiwhinn) is the teaching pastor at Shepherd's House Bible Church in Chandler, Arizona. His weekly sermons from Shepherd's House are available on YouTube (@shepherdshouseAZ) or at www.shepherdsaz.org. In addition to being a local pastor and author, Costi is the founder and president of For the Gospel, a resource ministry that provides sound doctrine for everyday people. For the Gospel reaches millions of people in more than 180 countries through videos, teaching series, podcasts, and social media content. Costi hosts the weekly *For the Gospel* podcast, available on Apple and Spotify or via video on YouTube. For the Gospel provides all its content for free and is supported by the generosity of ministry partners. Visit www.forthegospel.org and follow @forthegospelmin for sharable content on all social media outlets, including Instagram, TikTok, Facebook, X, and YouTube.

Sound Doctrine For Everyday People

+ +
+
+ +
+
+ +
+
+ +
+
+ +
+

For The Gospel is an online resource ministry founded by Costi Hinn focused on providing excellent content that's rooted in Scripture. For videos, podcasts, and articles on hundreds of theological topics, go to **www.forthegospel.org,** and follow For The Gospel on all social media platforms.

Knowing the Spirit
Who He Is, What He Does, and How He
Can Transform Your Christian Life
Costi W. Hinn

Using clear and sound interpretation of Scripture,
author, speaker, and pastor Costi Hinn addresses
common misconceptions and answers the most
frequently asked questions about who the Holy Spirit is and what
He does so you can begin to experience Him as a comforter, guide,
and source of power.

More Than a Healer
Not the Jesus You Want, but the Jesus
You Need
Costi W. Hinn

For a world desperate for healing, author and
pastor Costi Hinn presents *More Than a Healer*,
a profound and eloquent work offering biblical
answers about God's healing power, wisdom for holding on to faith
even in the most painful trials, and help for finding lasting hope in a
deep relationship with the Healer Himself.

God, Greed, and the
(Prosperity) Gospel
How Truth Overwhelms a Life Built
on Lies
Costi W. Hinn

Costi Hinn went from being a next-generation
preacher in a prosperity gospel dynasty to aban-
doning the family faith for the true gospel. *God, Greed, and the
(Prosperity) Gospel* offers unprecedented perspective on the perils
of greed, threats to the global church, and encouragement for your
own journey toward the Truth.